BRUNO GMÜNDER ■ EDITION EUROS

PO Box 11 07 29
10837 Berlin
Germany
Phone: ++49 (30) 615 00 30

This book was originally published under the title
Desert Patrol by Alternative Books, R.S.A.
Styling by GERHARDT
Lithography: Rainbow Graphics
Production: Michael Taubenheim
Printing: Heenemann
Printed in Germany
ISBN 3-86187-075-4

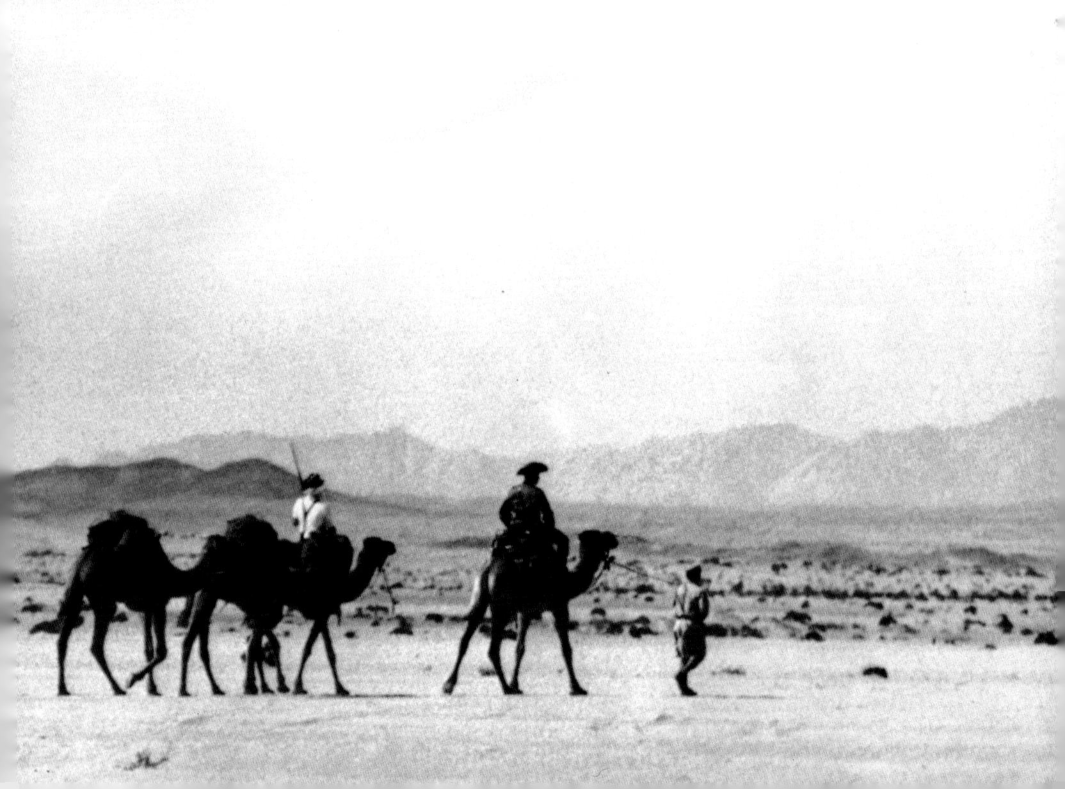

EDITION EUROS 6

DESERT PATROL

Photographs by Dook

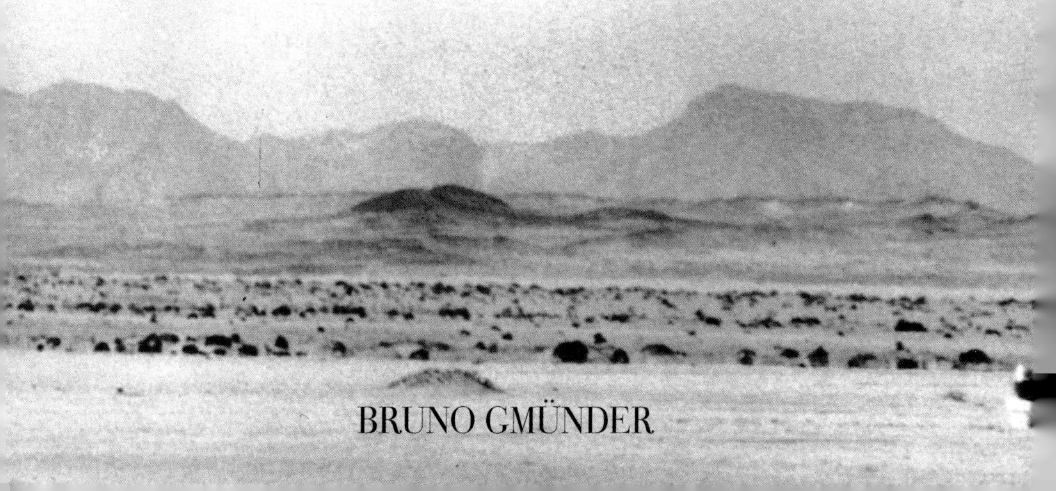

BRUNO GMÜNDER

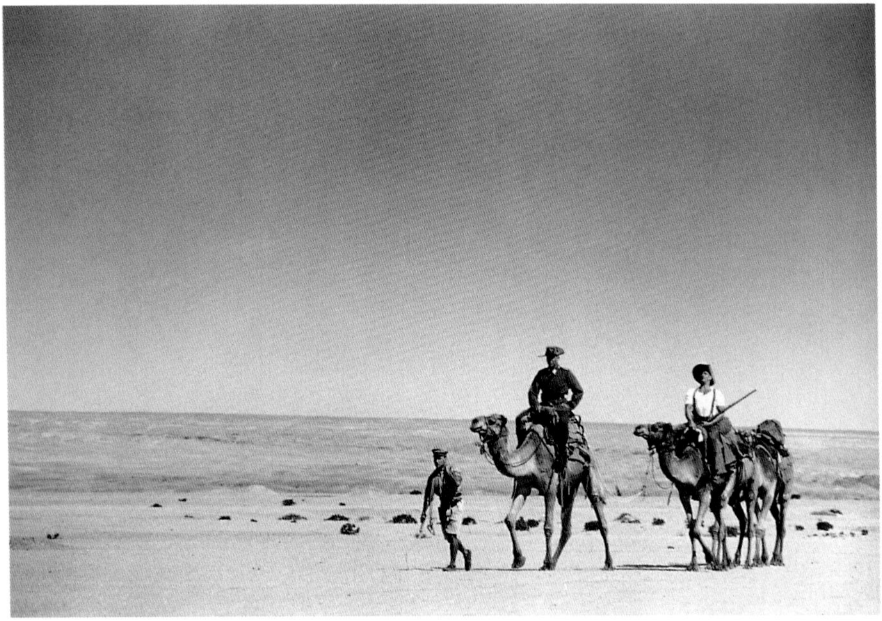

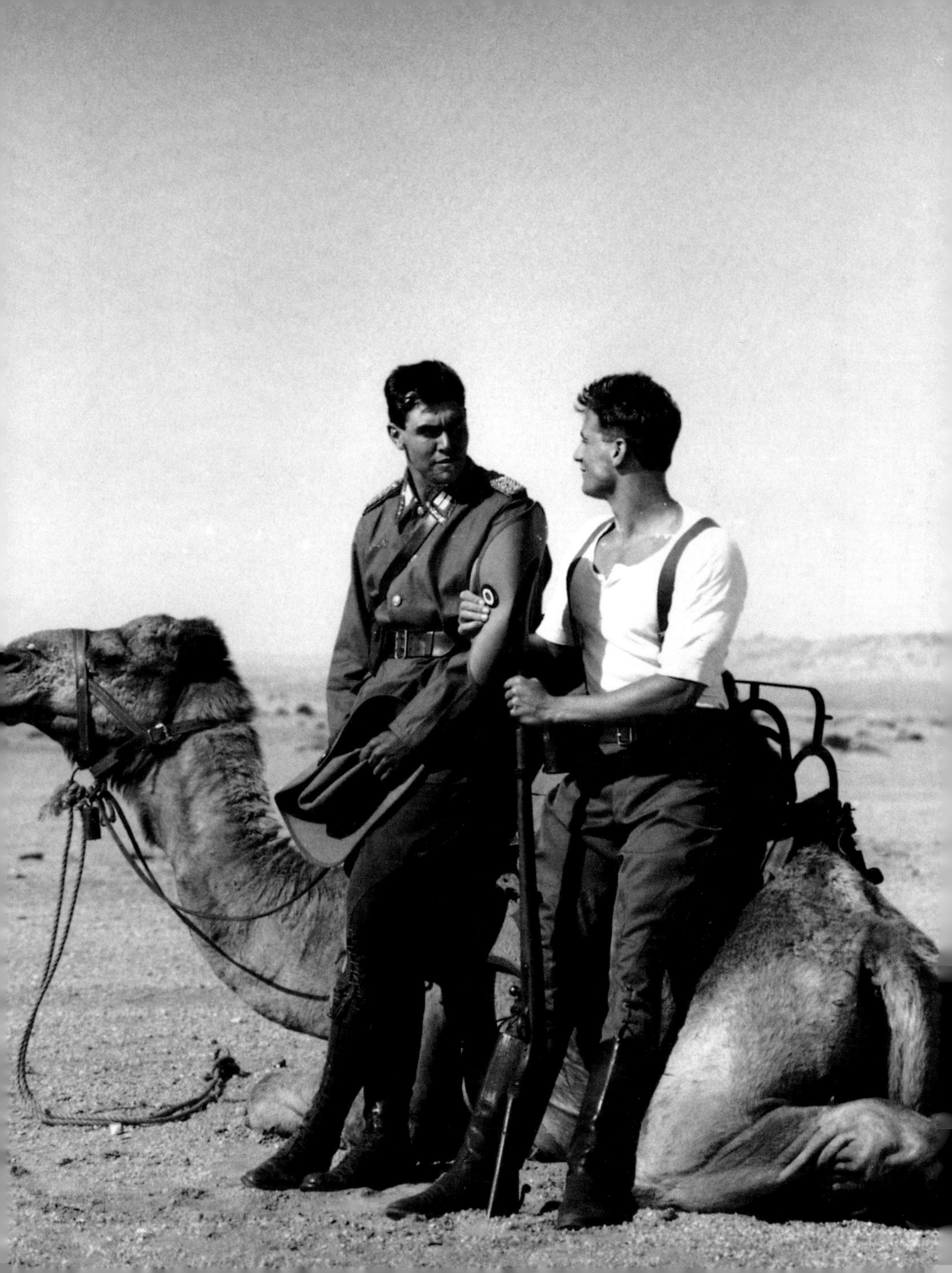

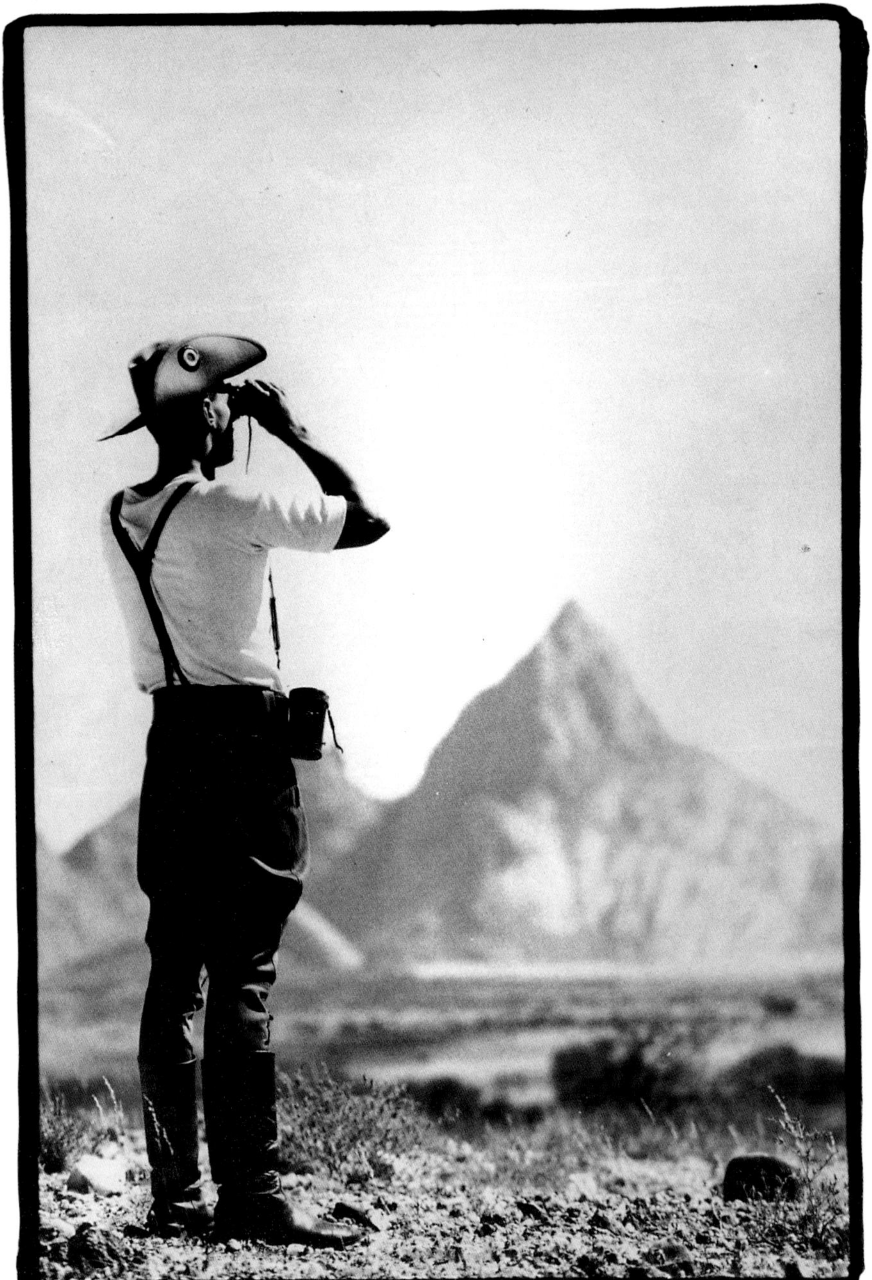

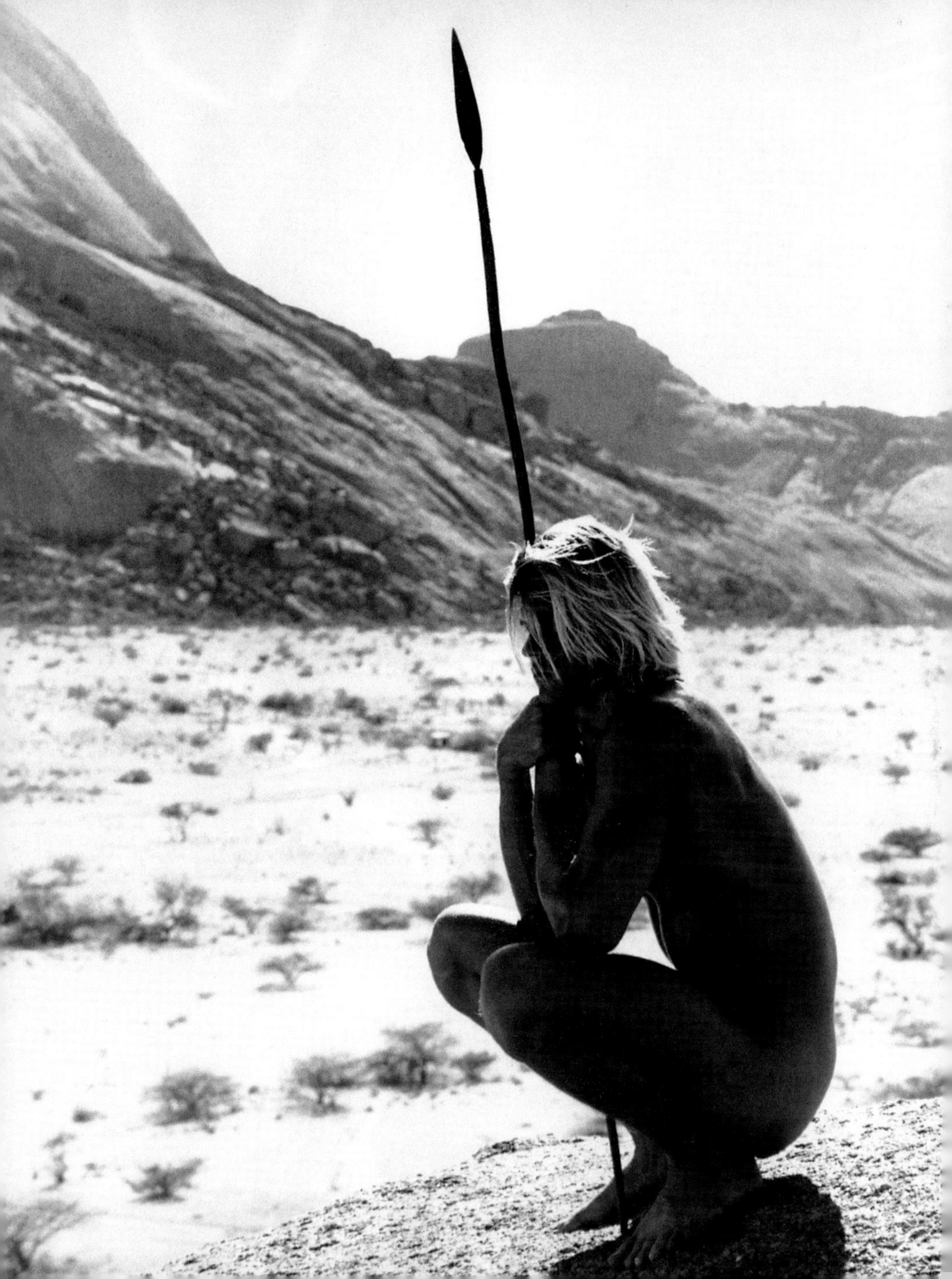

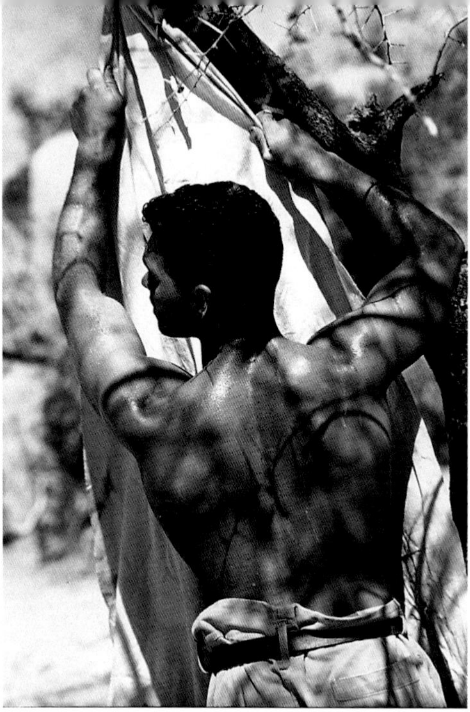

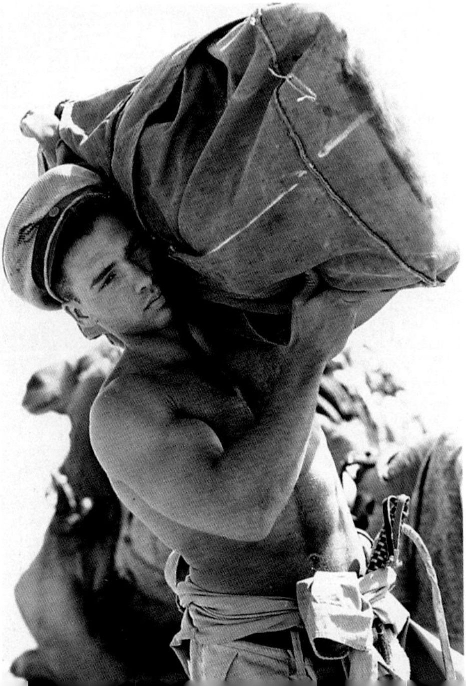

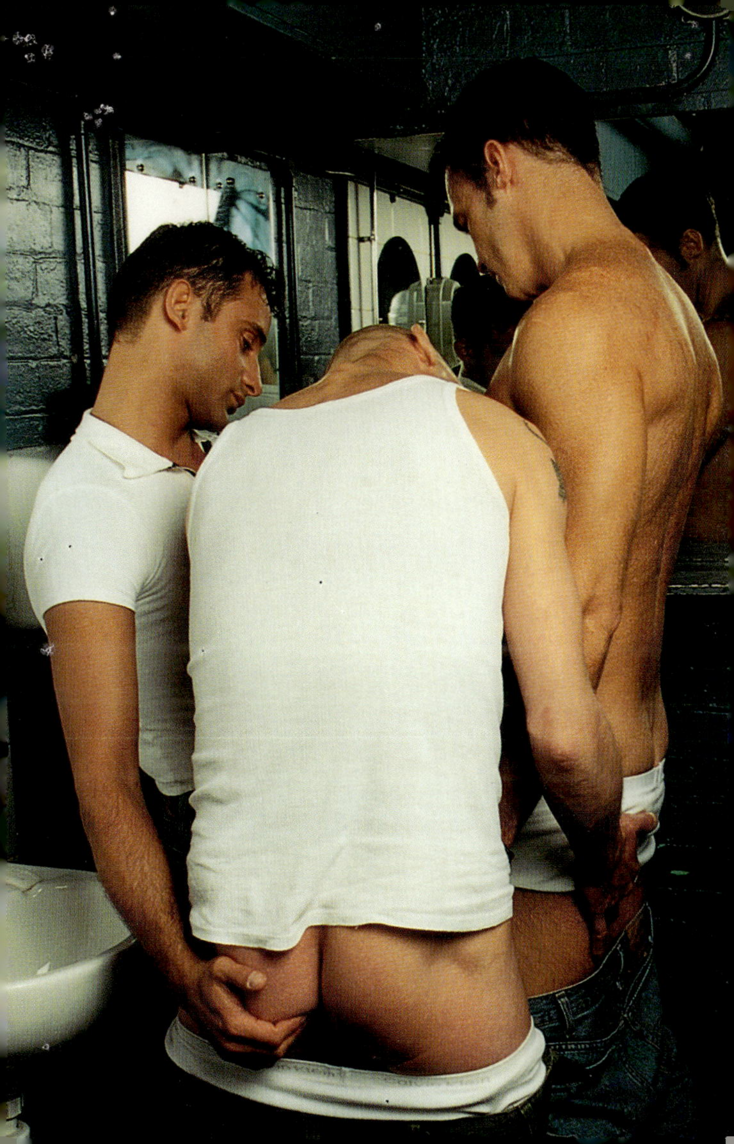

Well how do you define monogamy?

... Rod said "I'm only going three days". How could he leave me for that long? Sod! I packed his condoms, his lube, his shaving stuff, his toothbrush... The man can't pack.

He came back and had that look in his eye. Hmm, I thought "who did he fuck?" I unpacked: no condoms and a new tube of lube, half used. At least he was careful. It was a kid of about 17, jammy bastard! And he's the one who says "we've been together this long, don't you think we should stop using condoms? Still, he's only human.

Me and John ended up on the Heath on Tuesday. A guy there gave me the greatest blowjob. I mentioned fucking. He said "I only have sex with my boyfriend" - weird eh?

You asked if I was monogamous. You know I only love Rod and I wouldn't have stayed with him this long if I wasn't, would I?

xxx
Jimmy.

If you want to get involved in GMFA or make a donation contact: GMFA

Freepost (SW 8526)
London SW2 1BR
Tel: 0171-738 6872

GMFA
Gay Men Fighting AIDS

Illustration by Den©

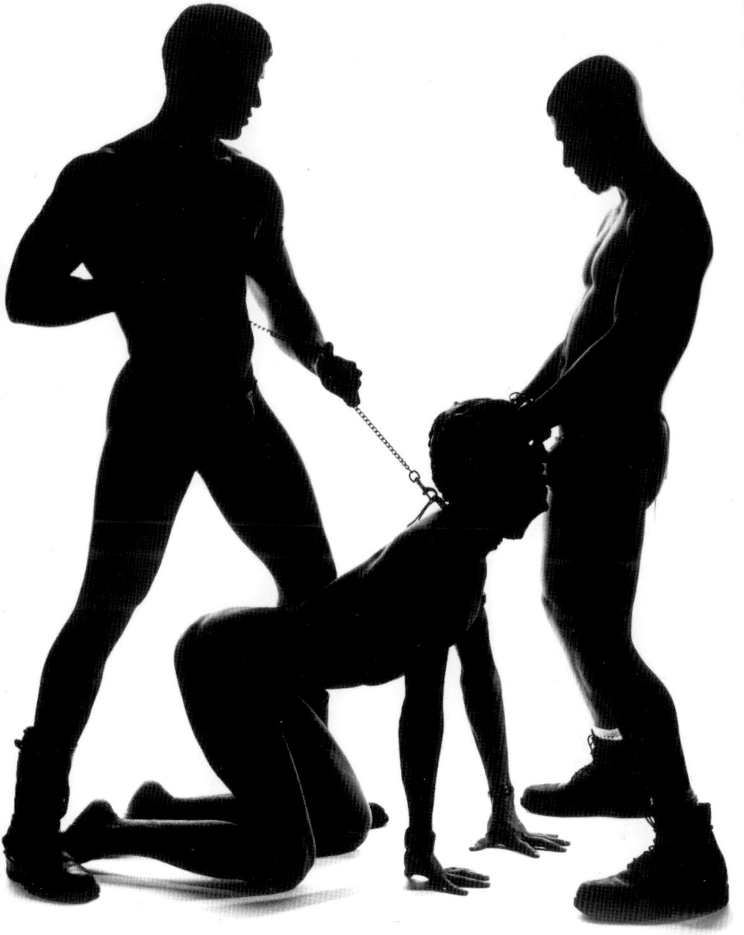

PLACE
STAMP
HERE

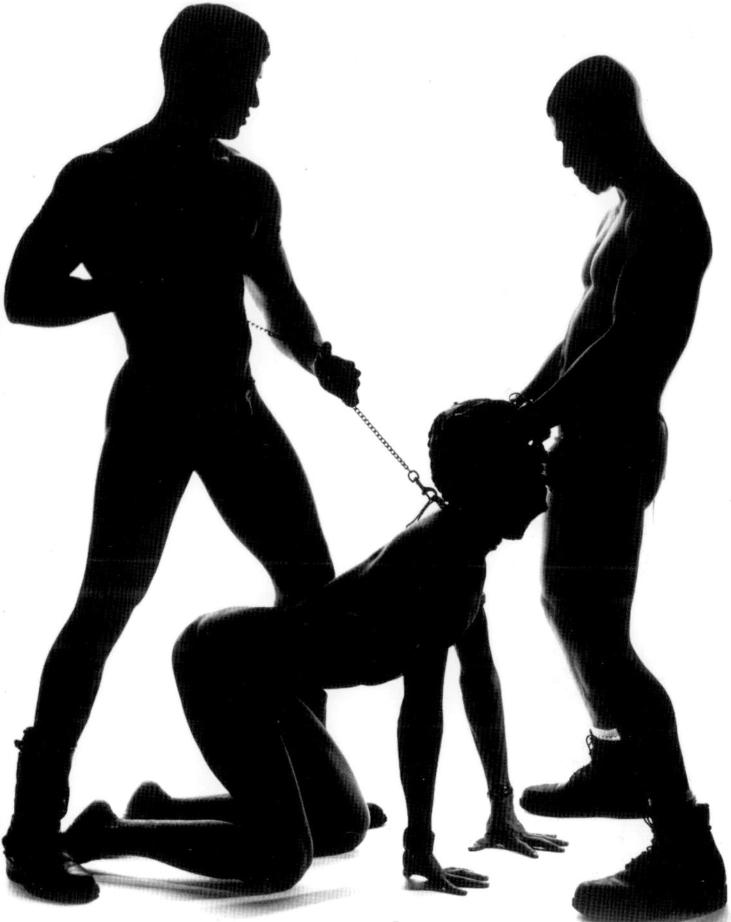

PLACE STAMP HERE

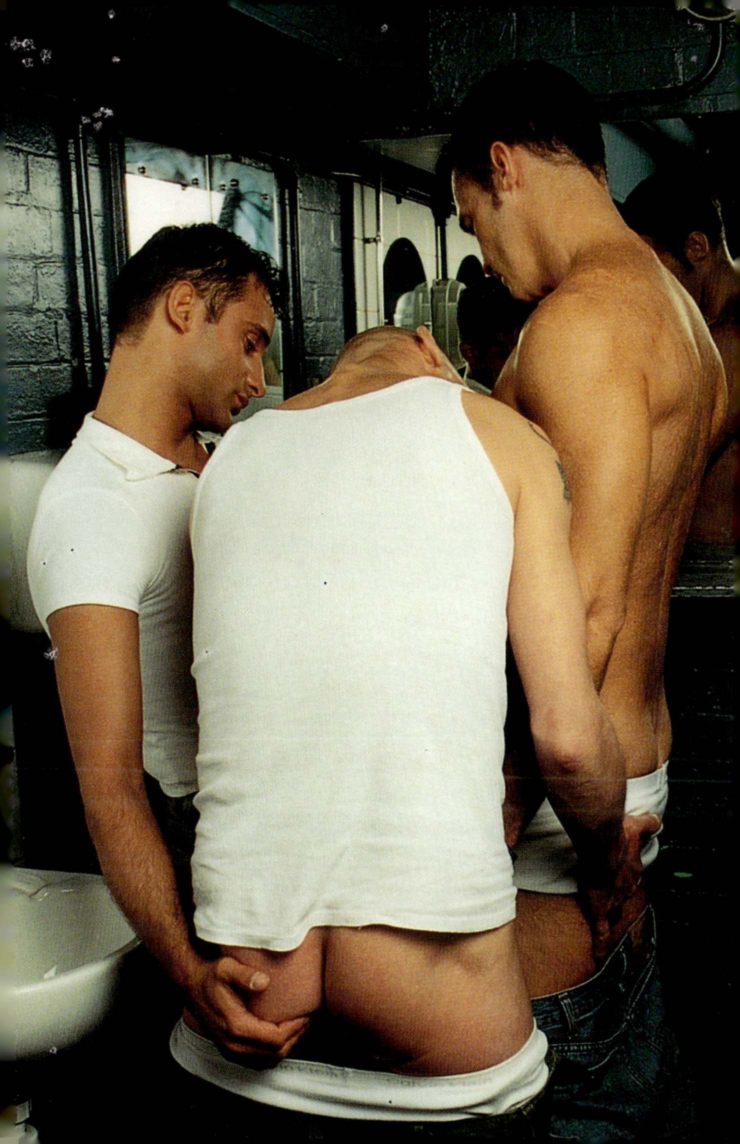

Well how do you define monogamy?

... Rod said "I'm only going three days". How could he leave me for that long? Sod! I packed his condoms, his lube, his shaving stuff, his toothbrush... The man can't pack.

He came back and had that look in his eye. Hmm, I thought "who did he fuck?" I unpacked: no condoms and a new tube of lube, half used. At least he was careful. It was a kid of about 17, jammy bastard! And he's the one who says "we've been together this long, don't you think we should stop using condoms? Still, he's only human.

Me and John ended up on the Heath on Tuesday. A guy there gave me the greatest blowjob. I mentioned fucking. He said "I only have sex with my boyfriend" - weird eh?

You asked if I was monogamous. You know I only love Rod and I wouldn't have stayed with him this long if I wasn't, would I?

xxx
Jimmy.

If you want to get involved in GMFA or make a donation contact: GMFA

Freepost (SW 8526)
London SW2 1BR
Tel: 0171-738 6872

GMFA
Gay Men Fighting AIDS

Illustration by Den©

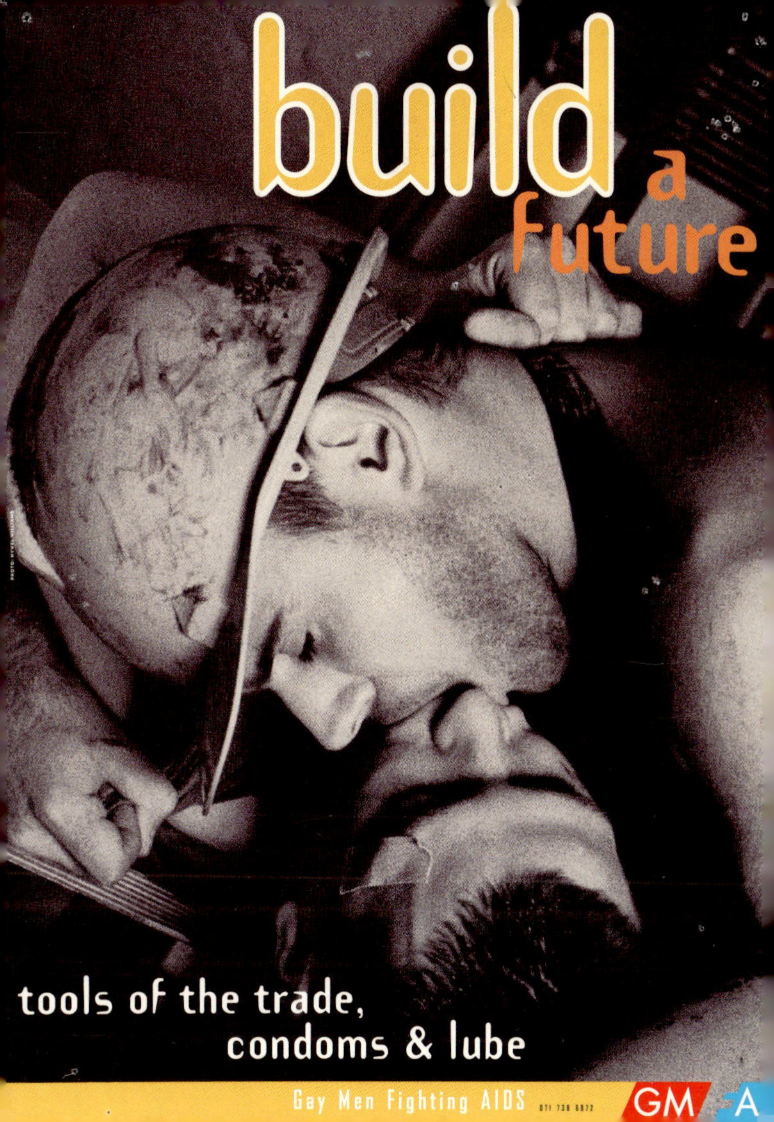
build a future
tools of the trade,
condoms & lube
Gay Men Fighting AIDS
071 738 6872
GMFA

Safer sex cuts down or cuts out the risks of getting or passing on HIV. The guidelines for safer sex are the same if you are HIV-positive, negative or don't know. Fucking without condoms is by far the biggest risk in sex. Extra strong condoms are best for anal sex - good ones are: Durex Ultra Strong, HT Specials, Mates Super Strong, and Gay Safe.

A condom on its own isn't enough - use lots of water-based lubricant such as KY, Liquid Silk, Slik and ForPlay. Never use oil-based lubes like vaseline as these rot the rubber really quickly and cause condoms to split. Don't rely on the other guy having some - take your own. It's easy to forget a condom in the heat of the moment - think and plan ahead and leave some by your bed.

Sucking is very much lower risk. Looking after your mouth and not getting cum in it reduces the risk even more. Kissing, wanking and any other forms of sex that don't involve blood and cum getting into the body are safe.

If you want to get involved in GMFA or make a donation contact:
Unit 42, 49 Effra Road, LONDON, SW2 1BZ. Tel: 071 738 6872

GMFA Gay Men Fighting AIDS

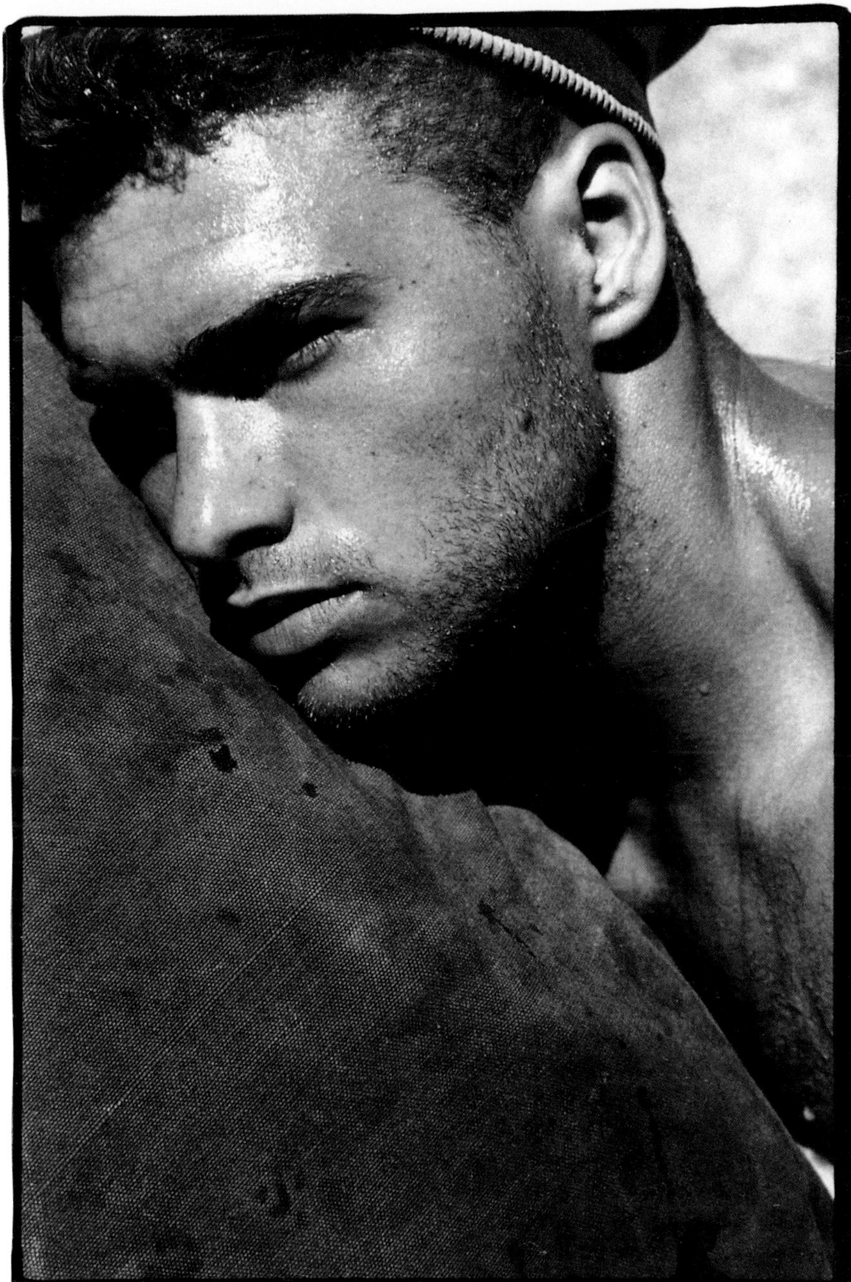

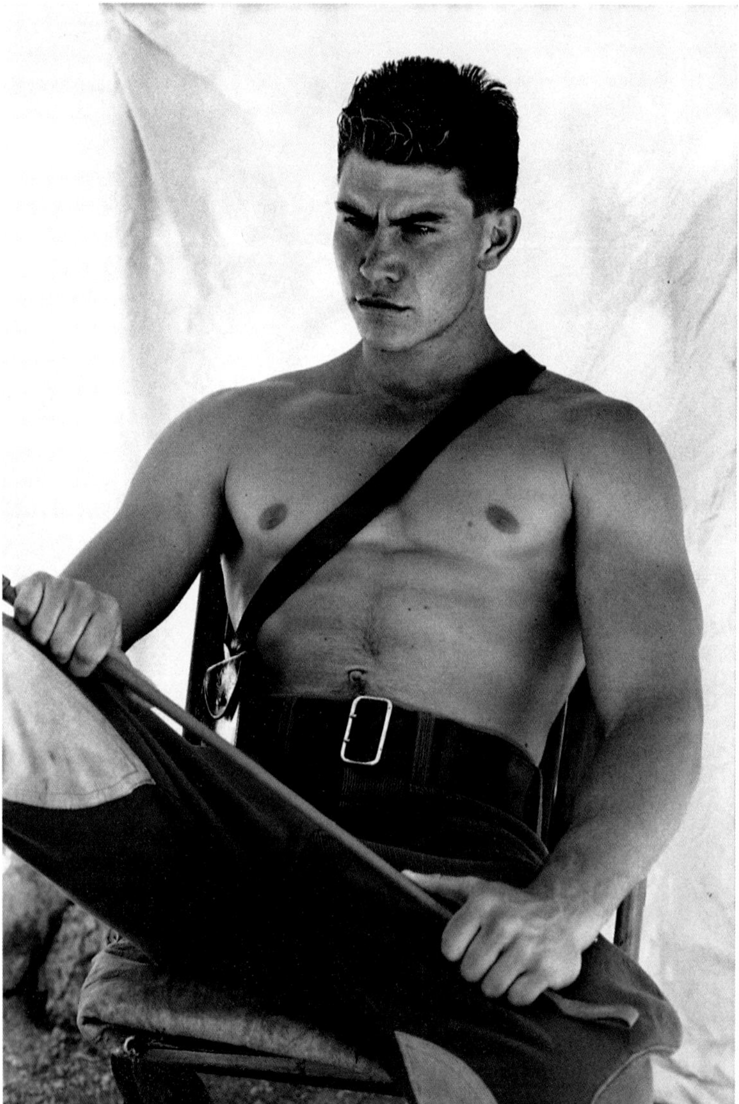

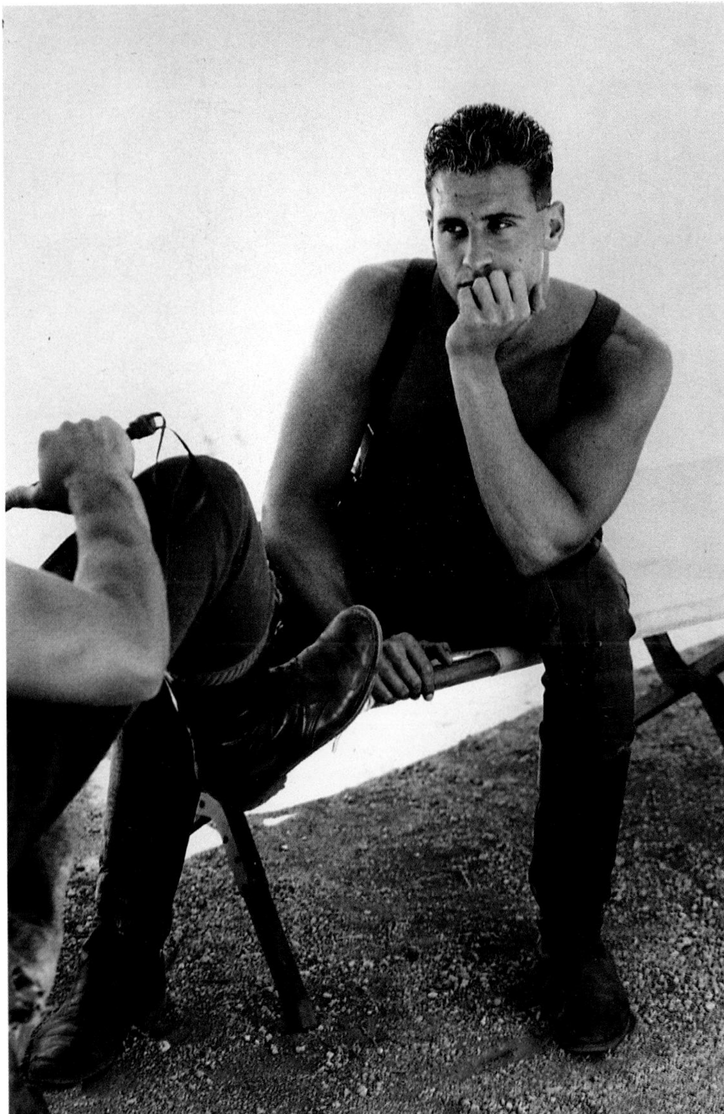

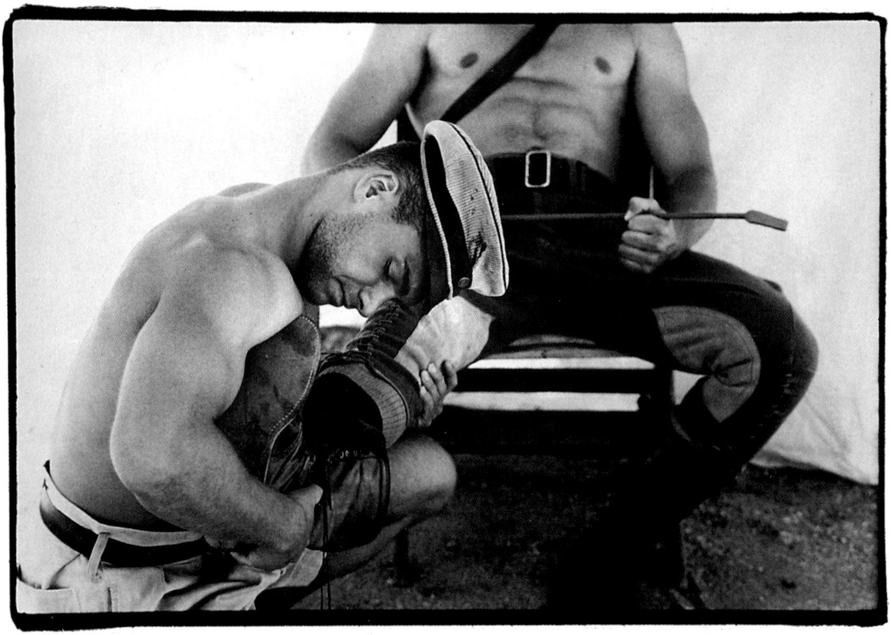

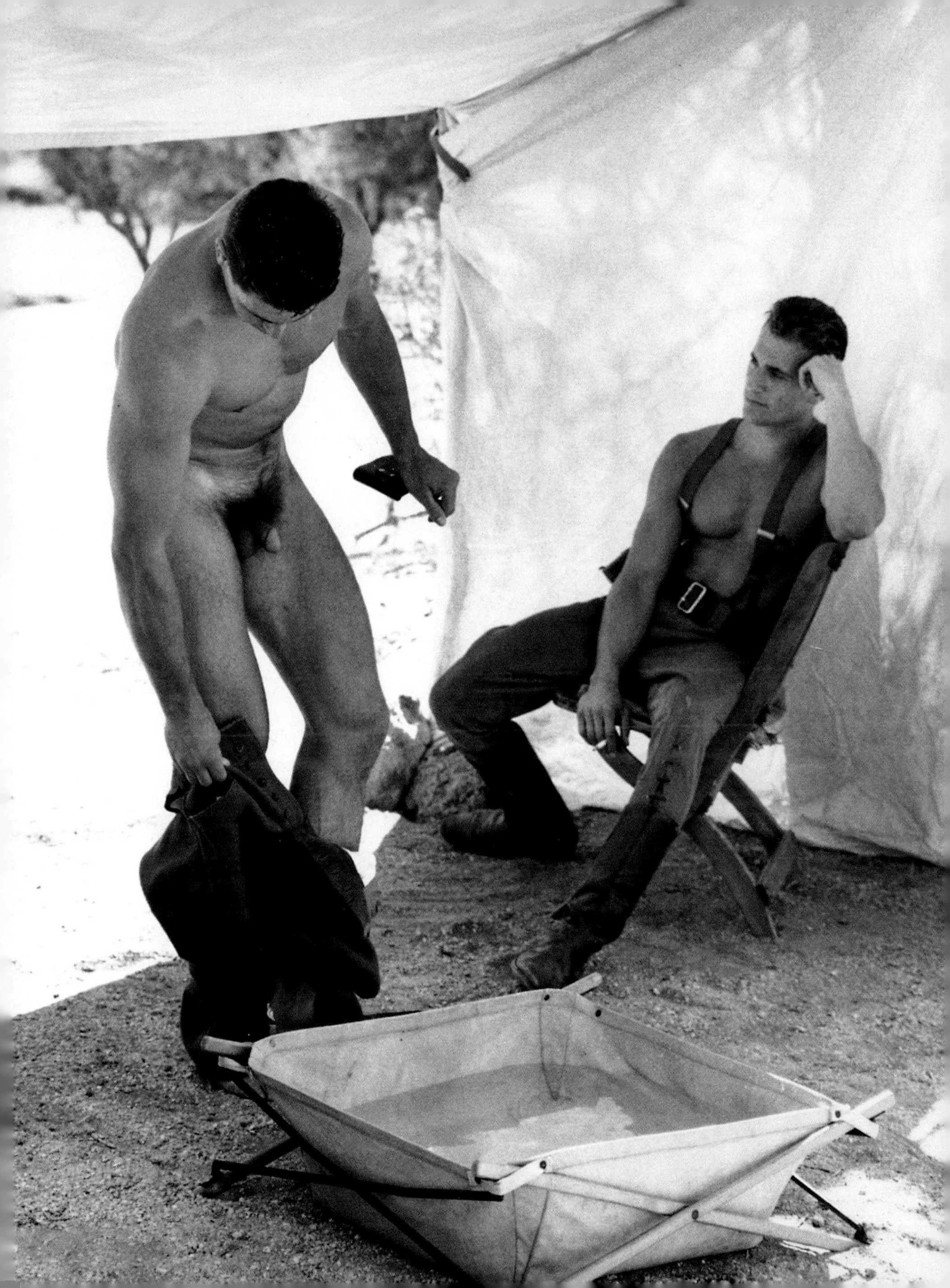

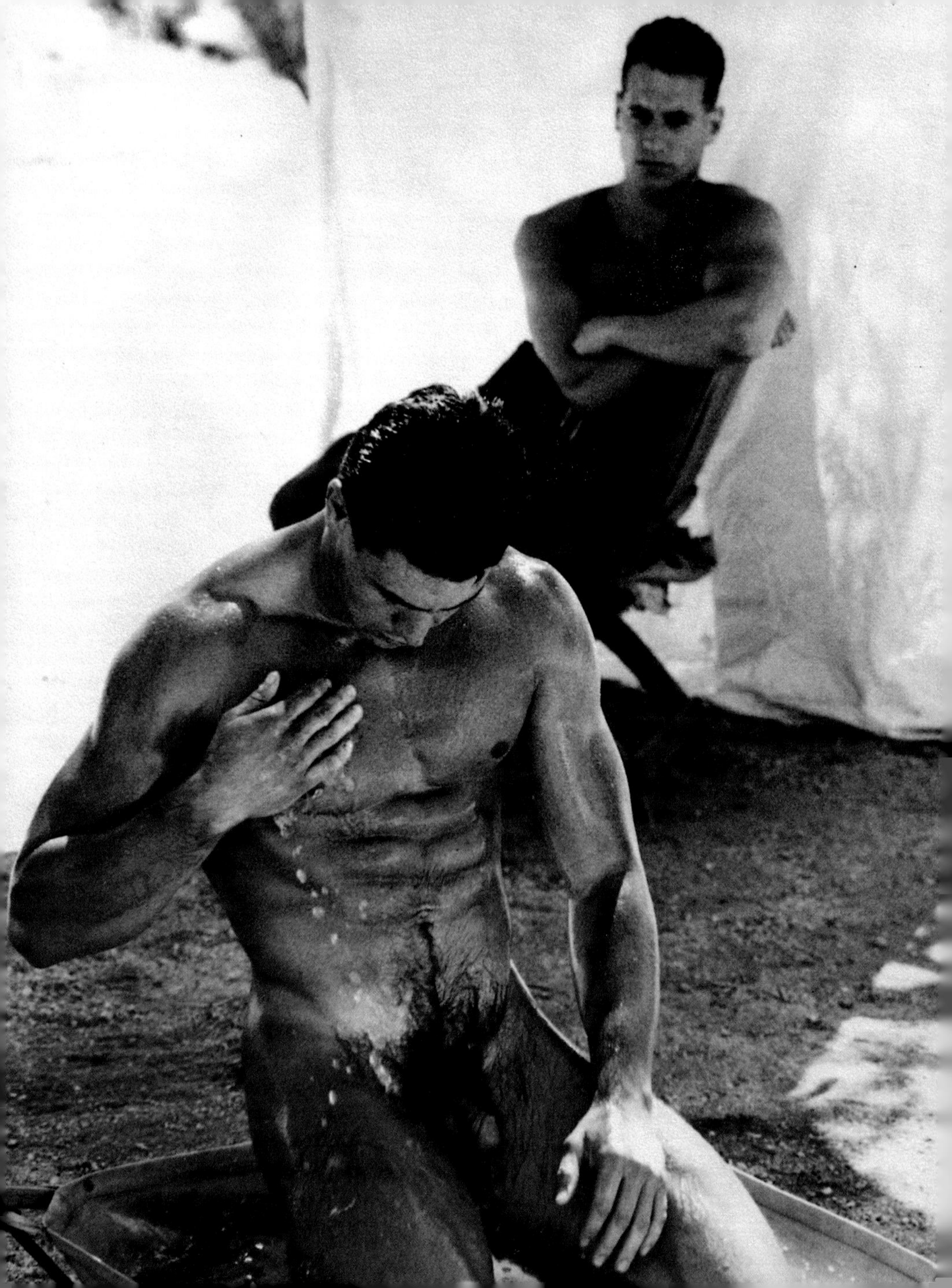

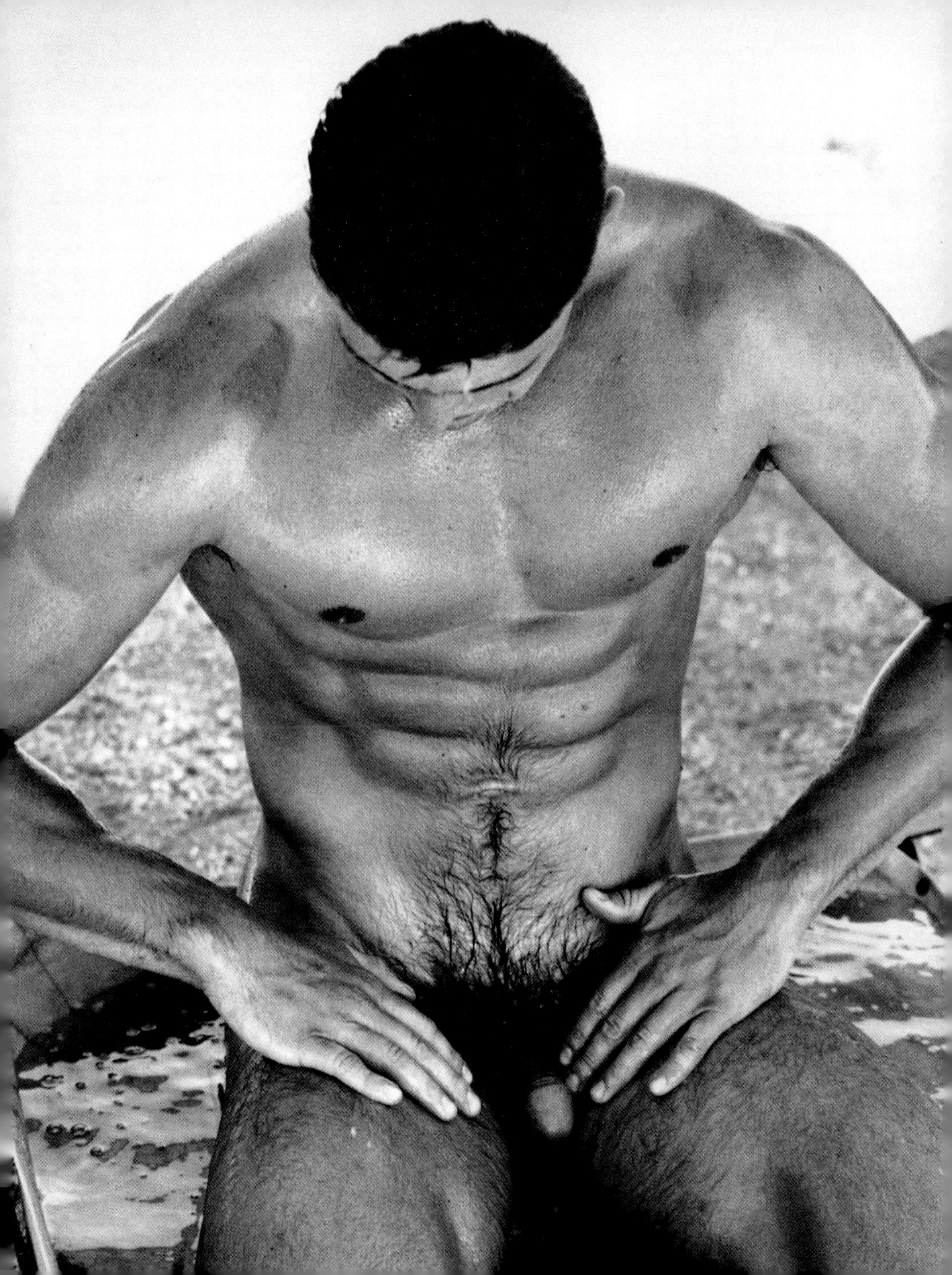

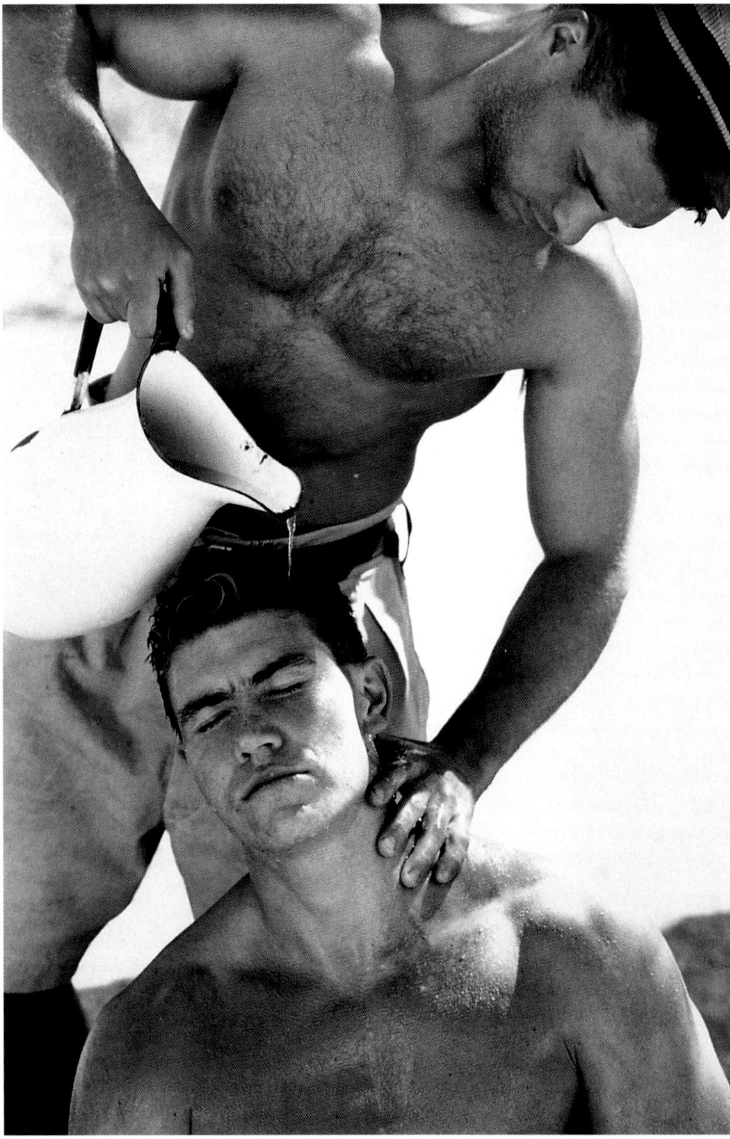

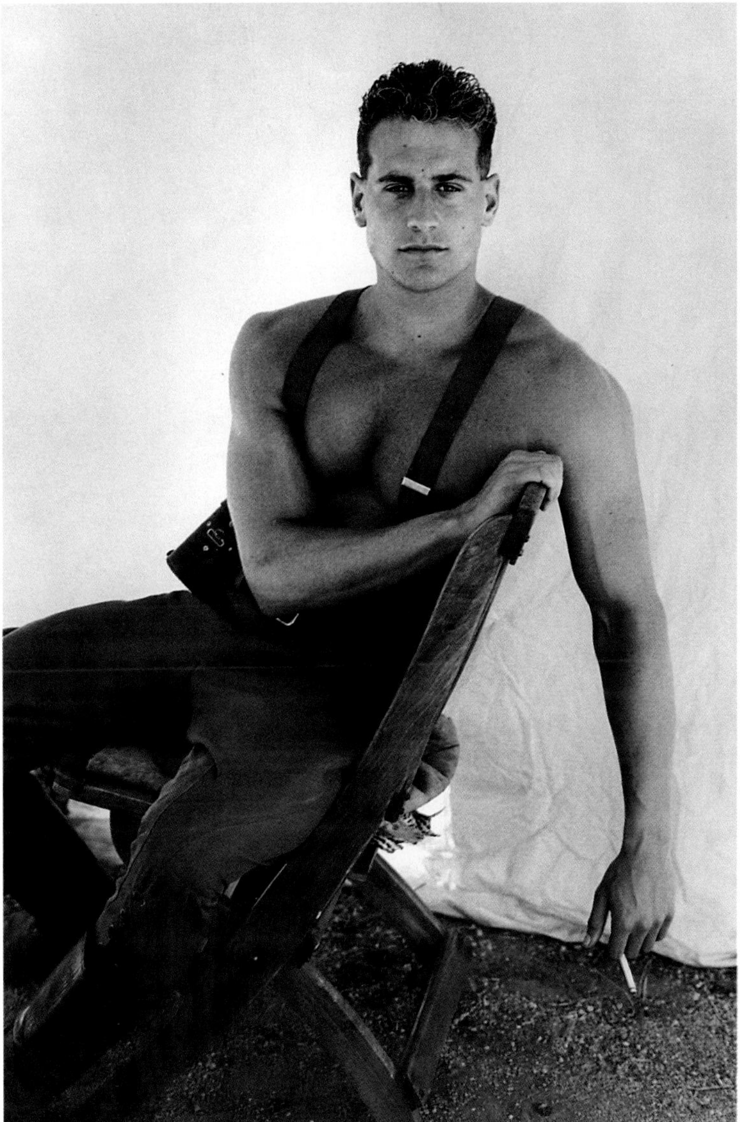

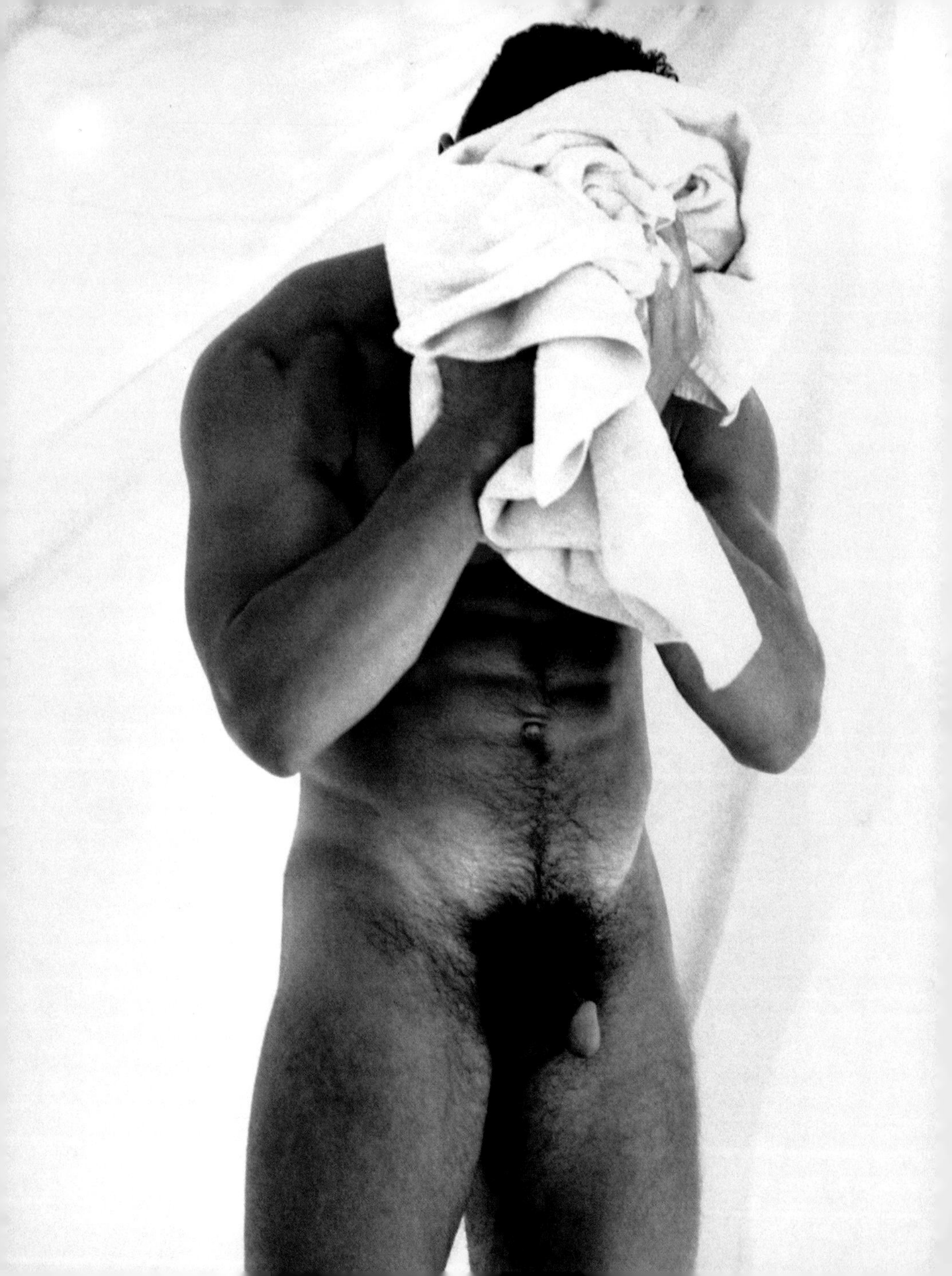

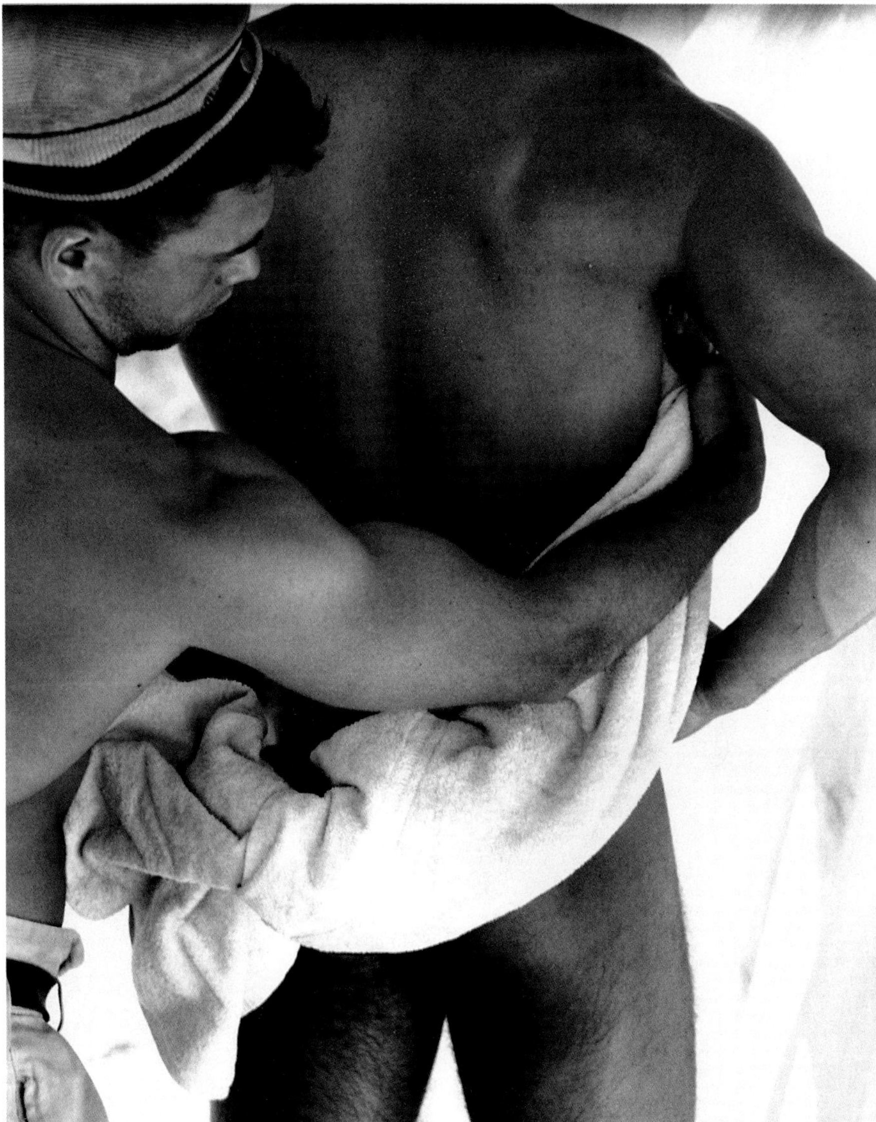

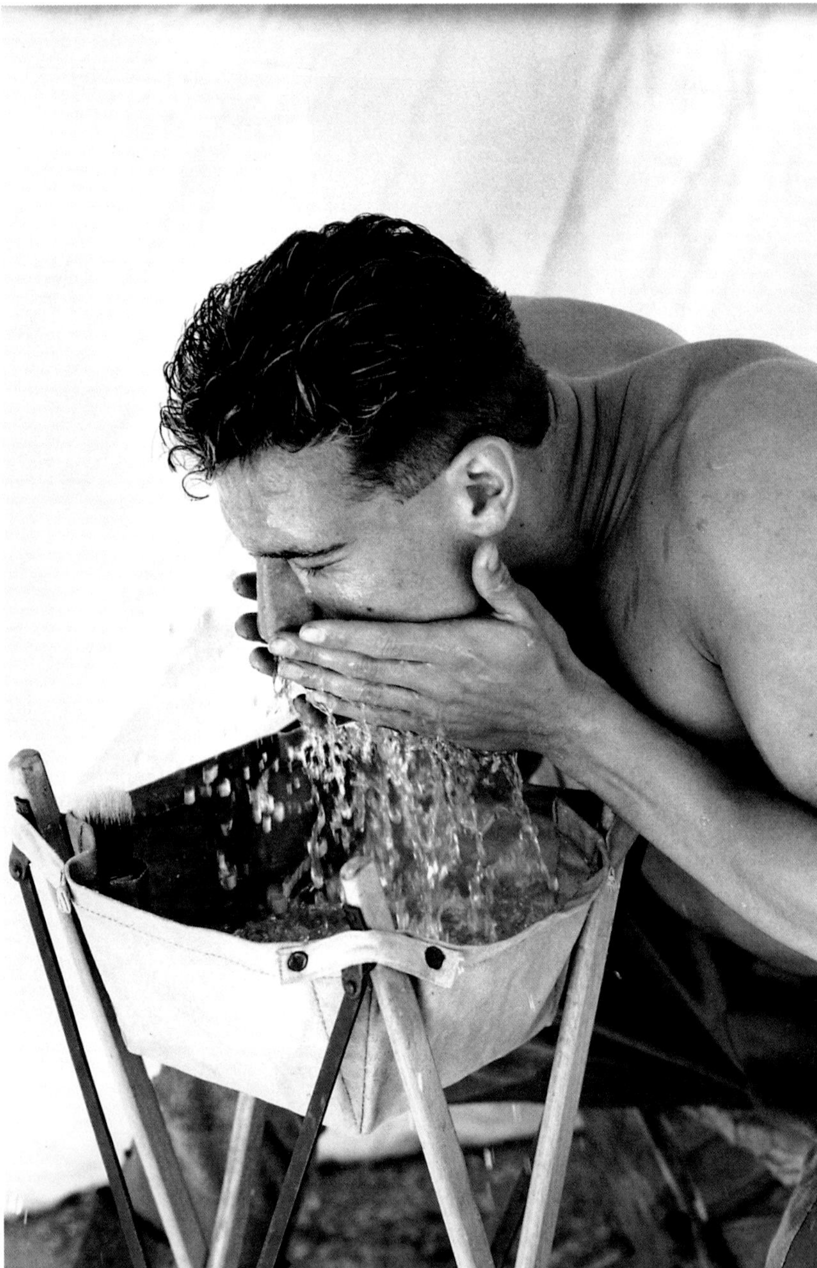

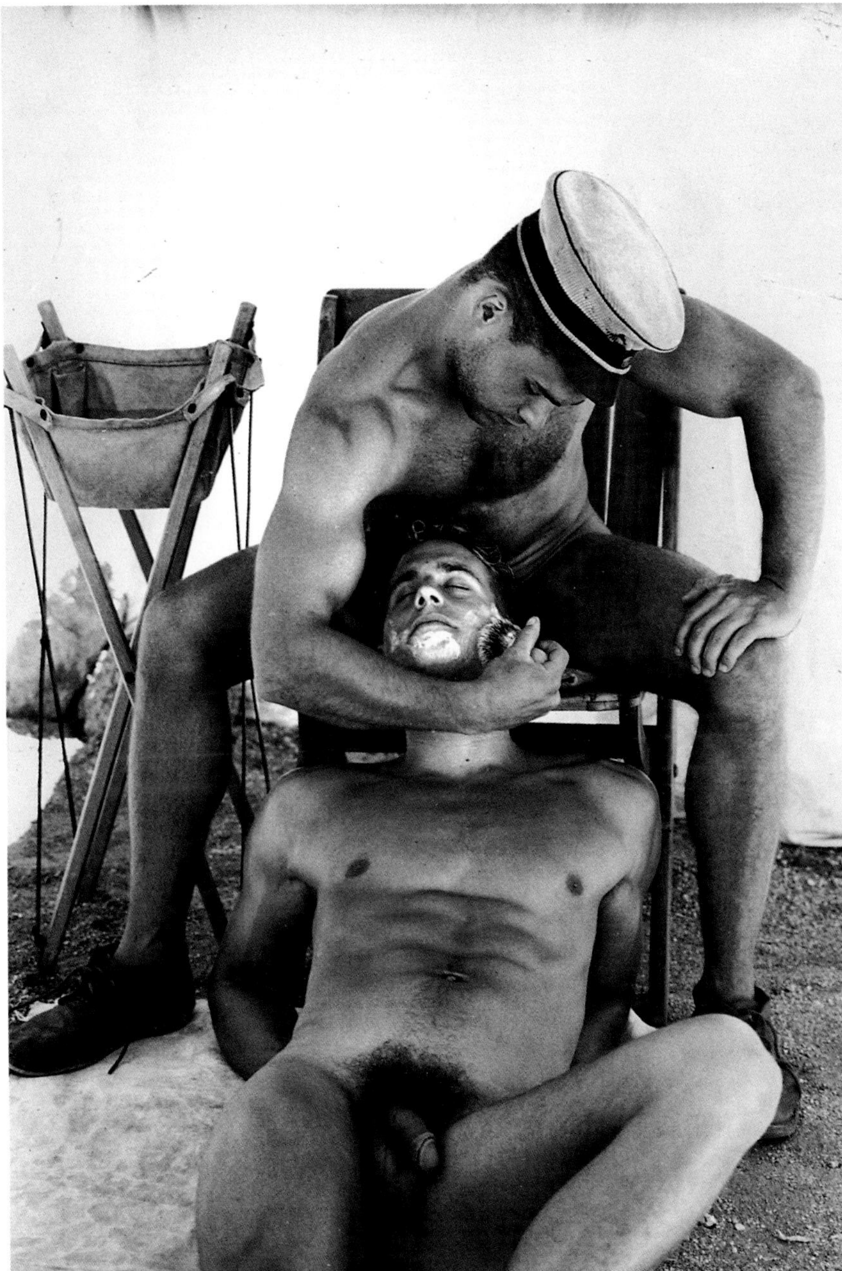

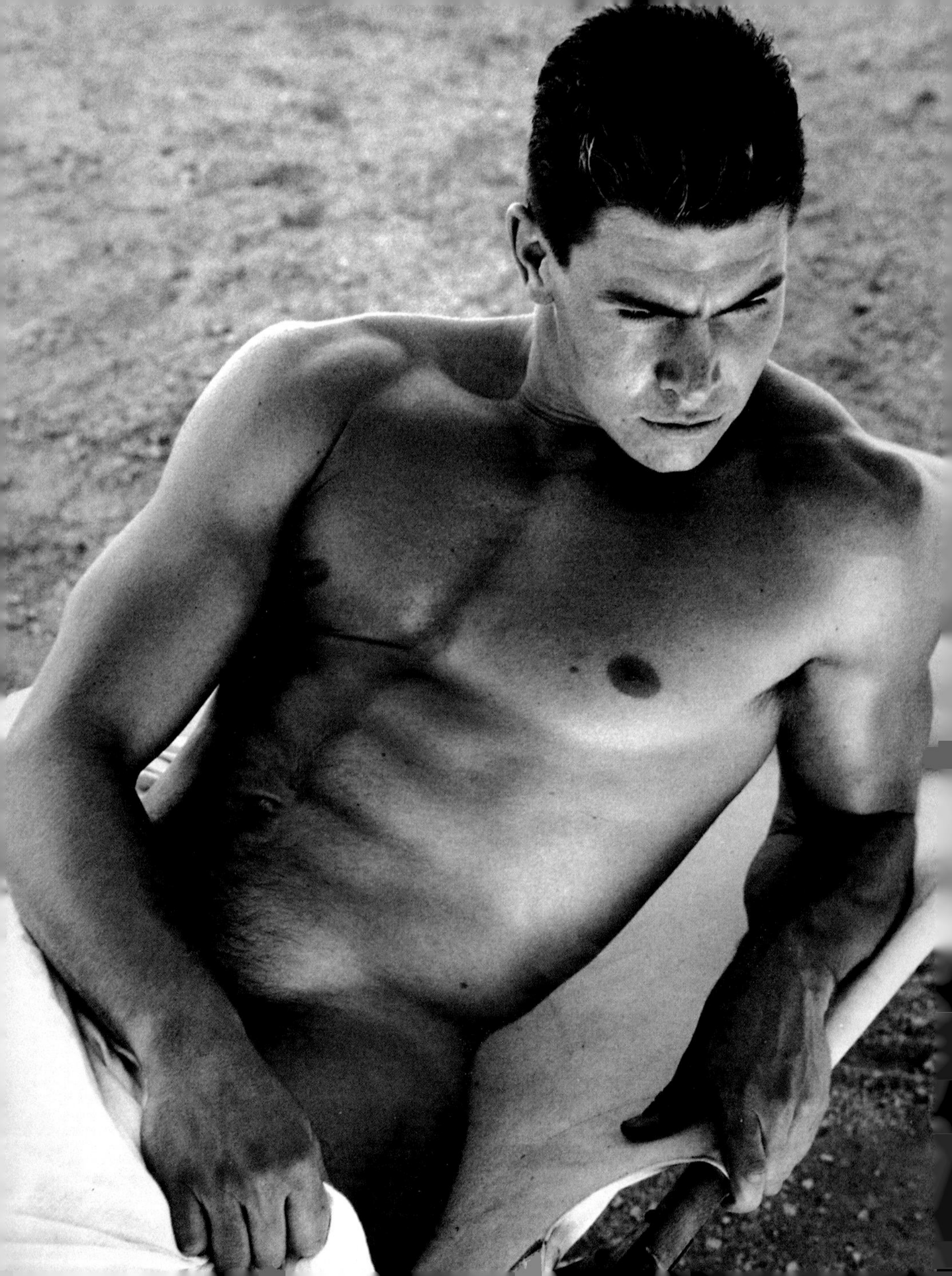

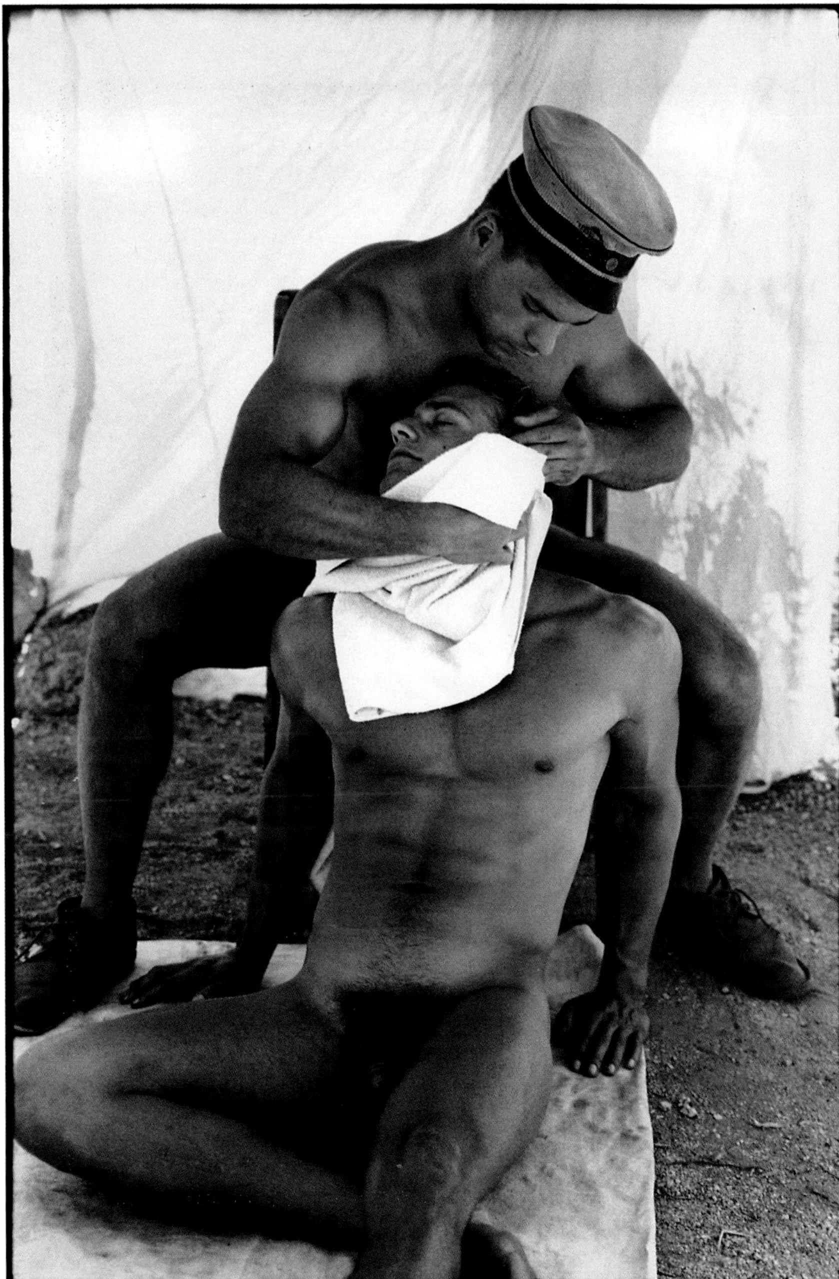

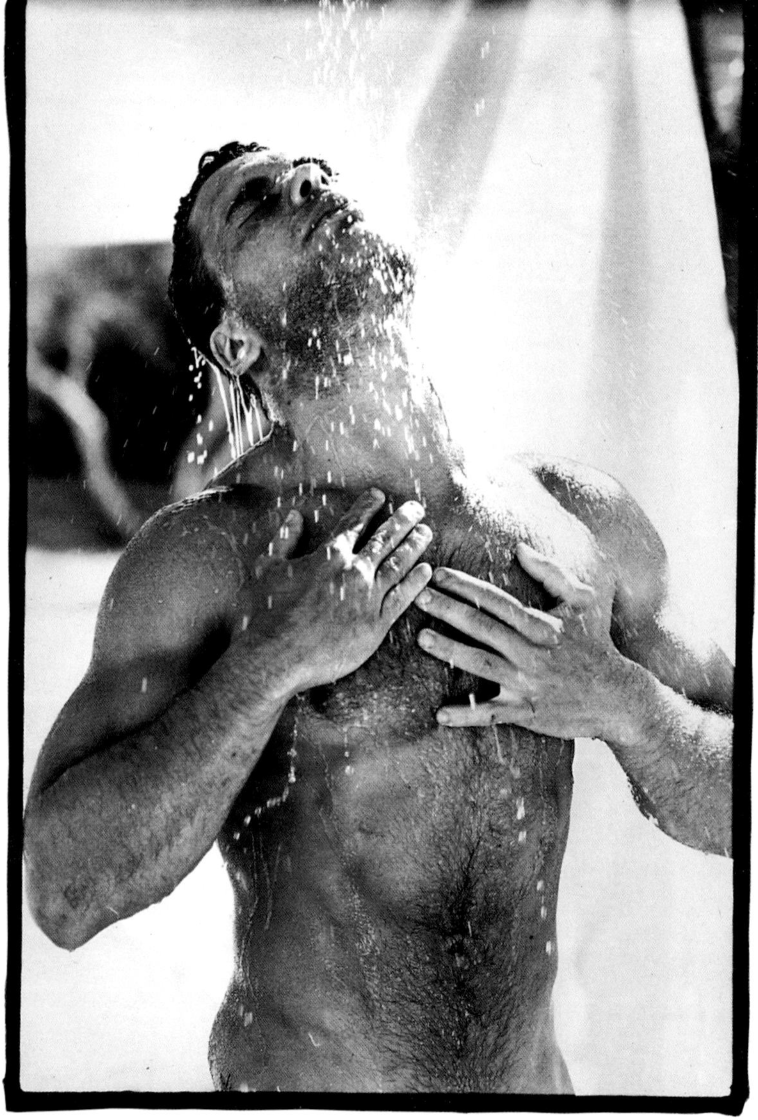

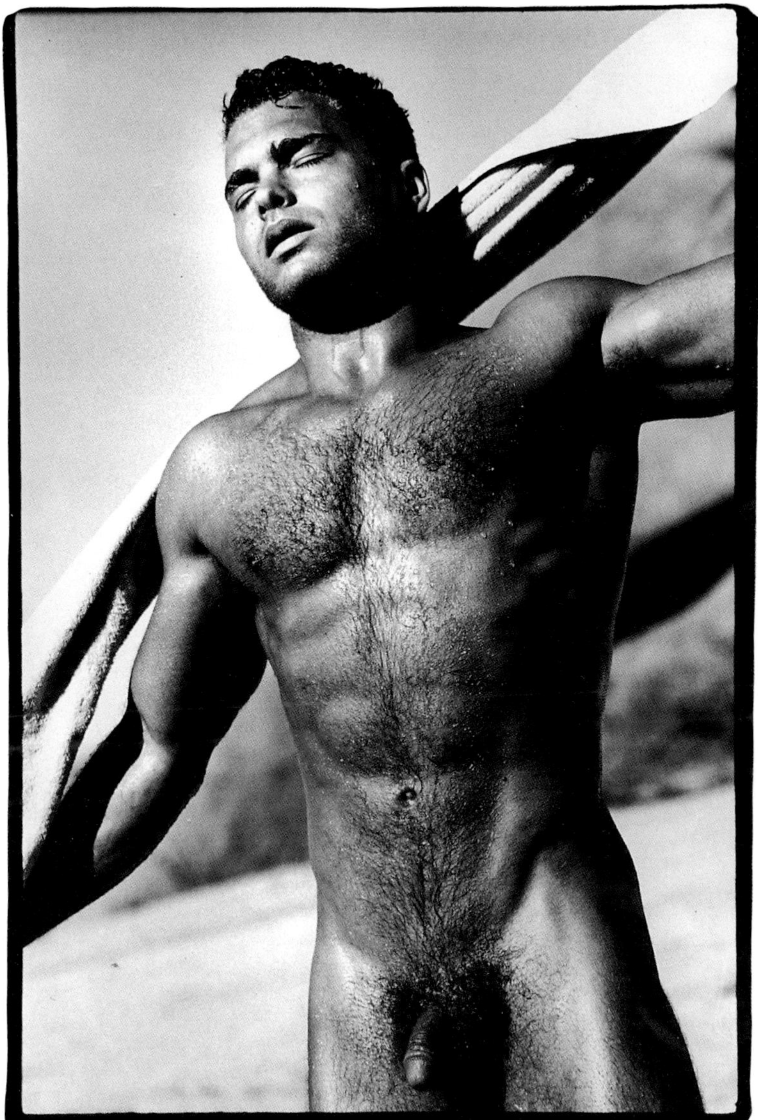

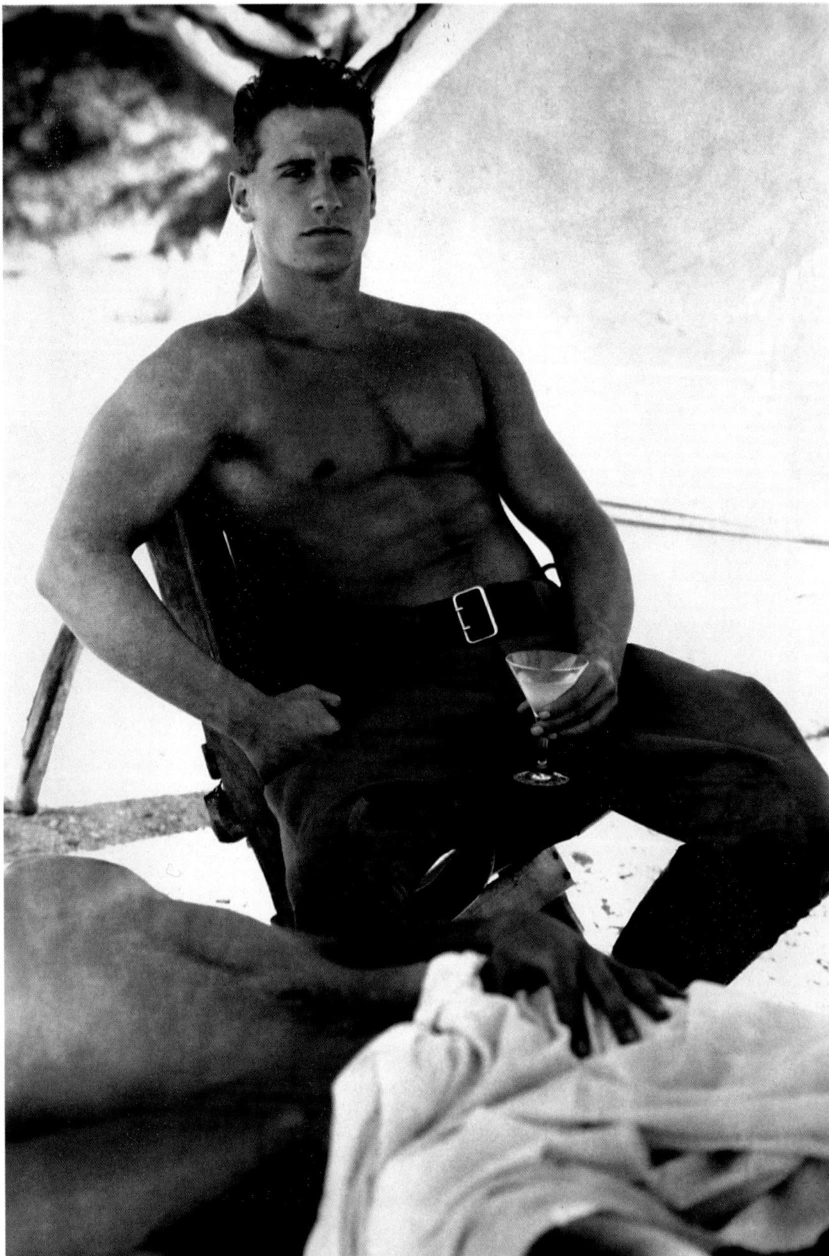

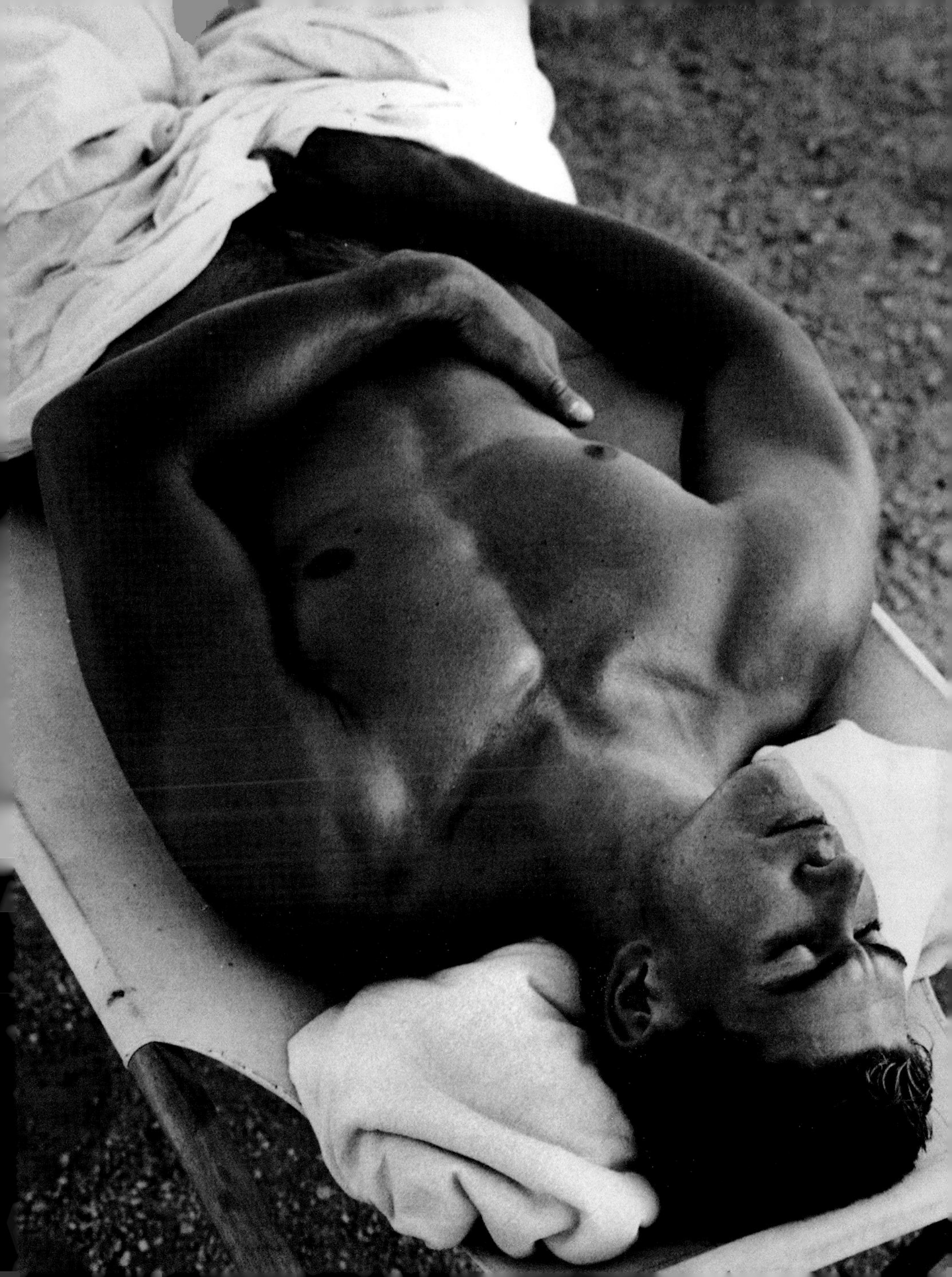

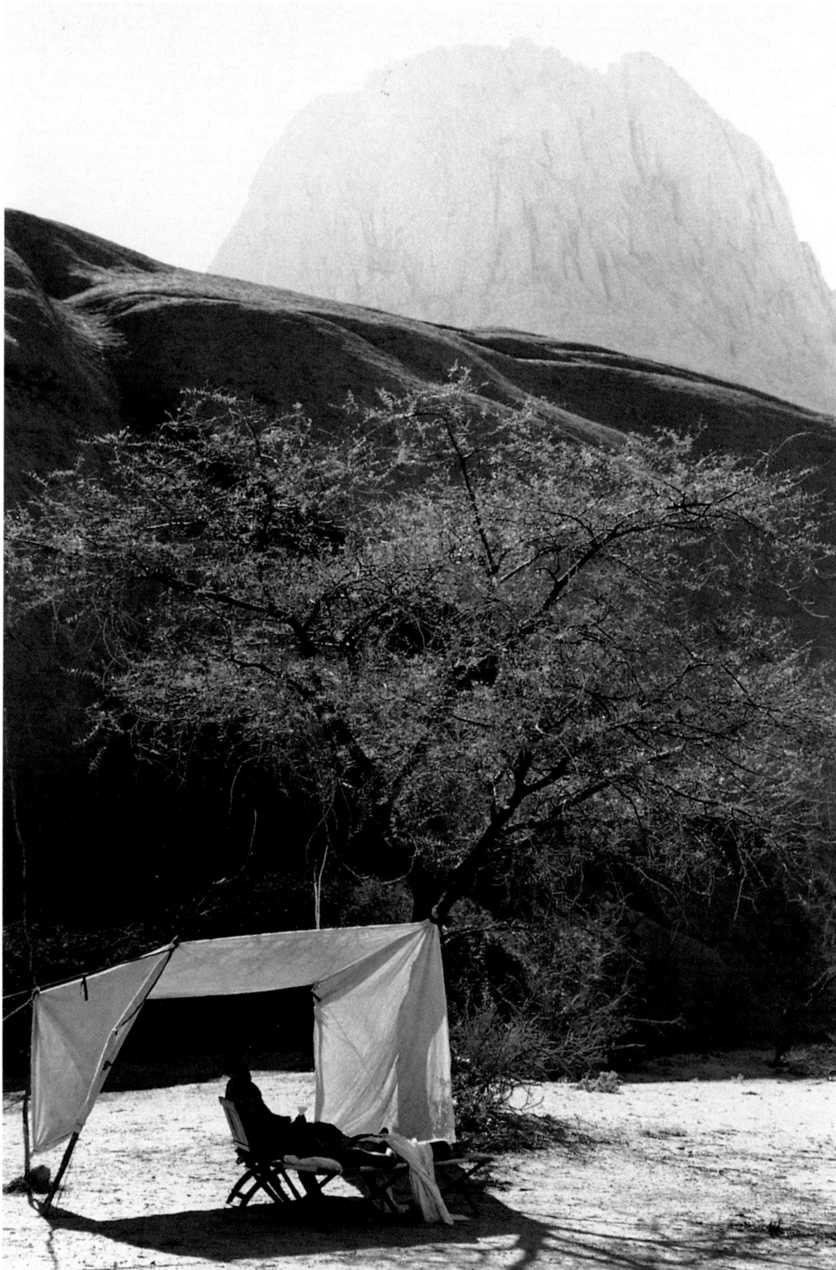

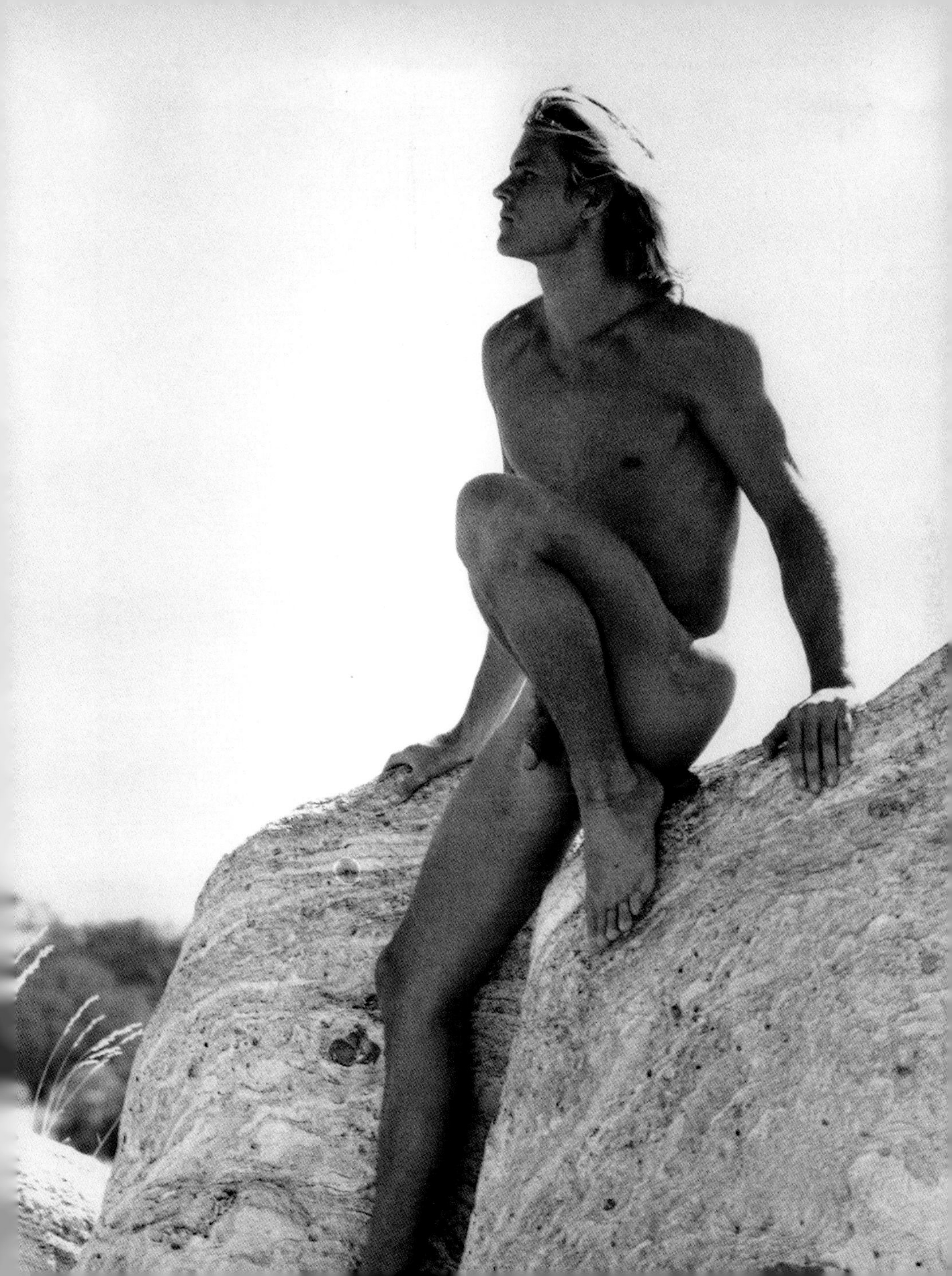

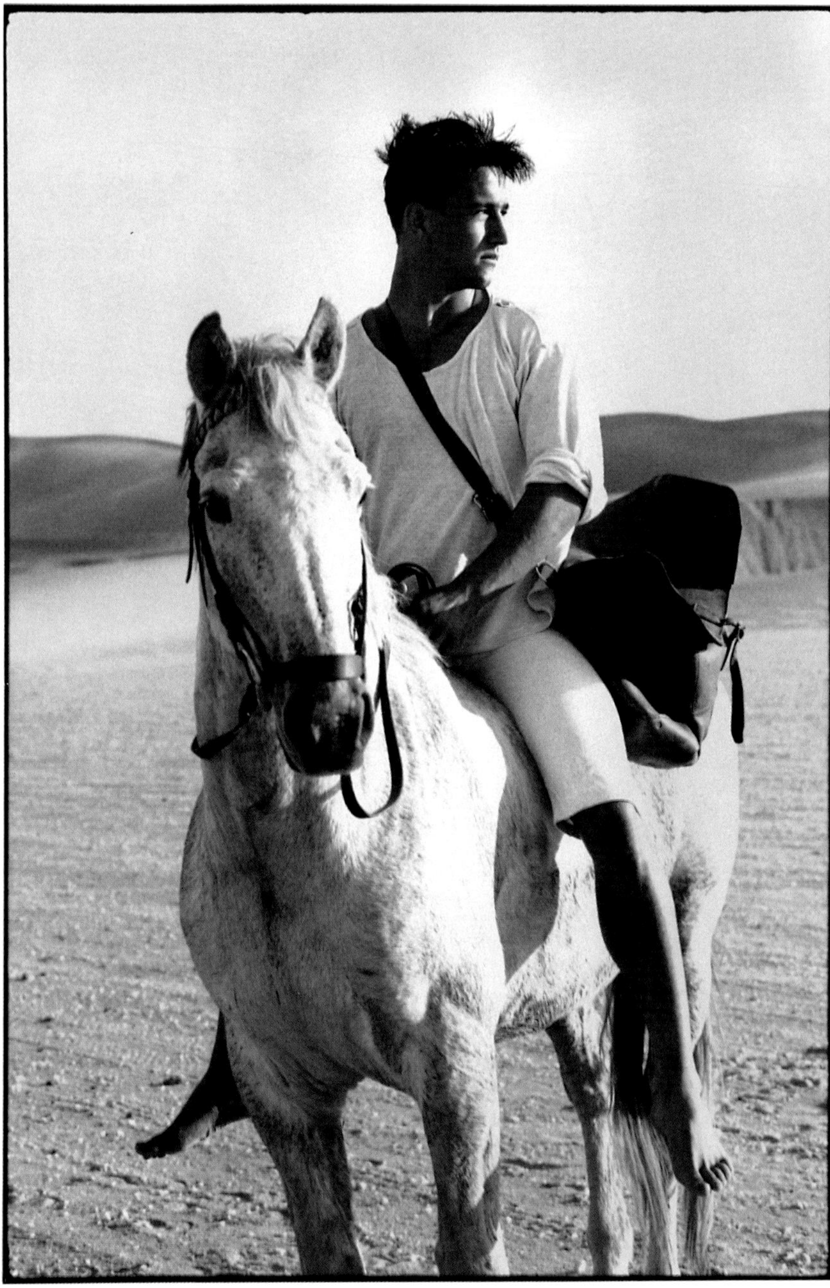

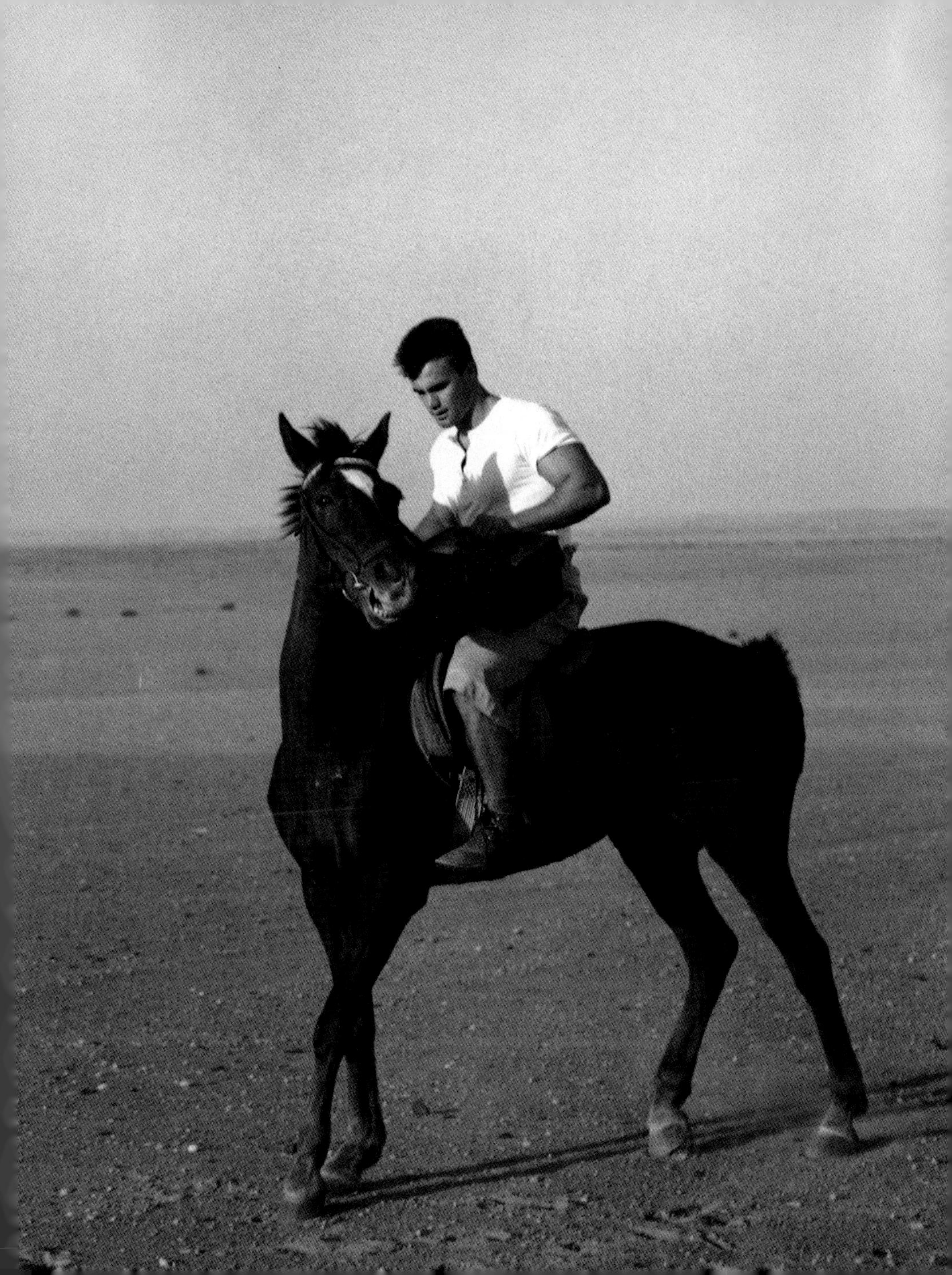

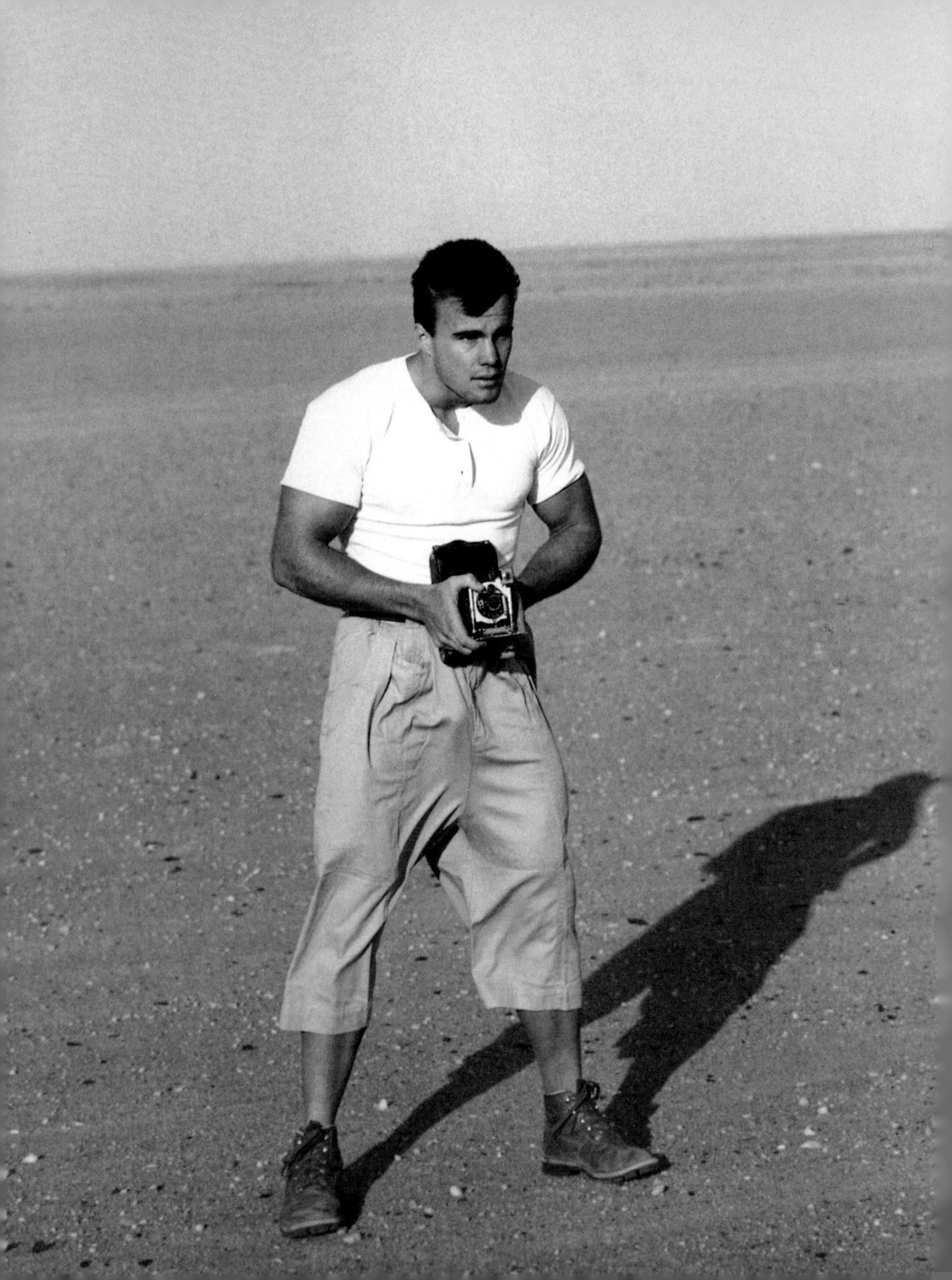

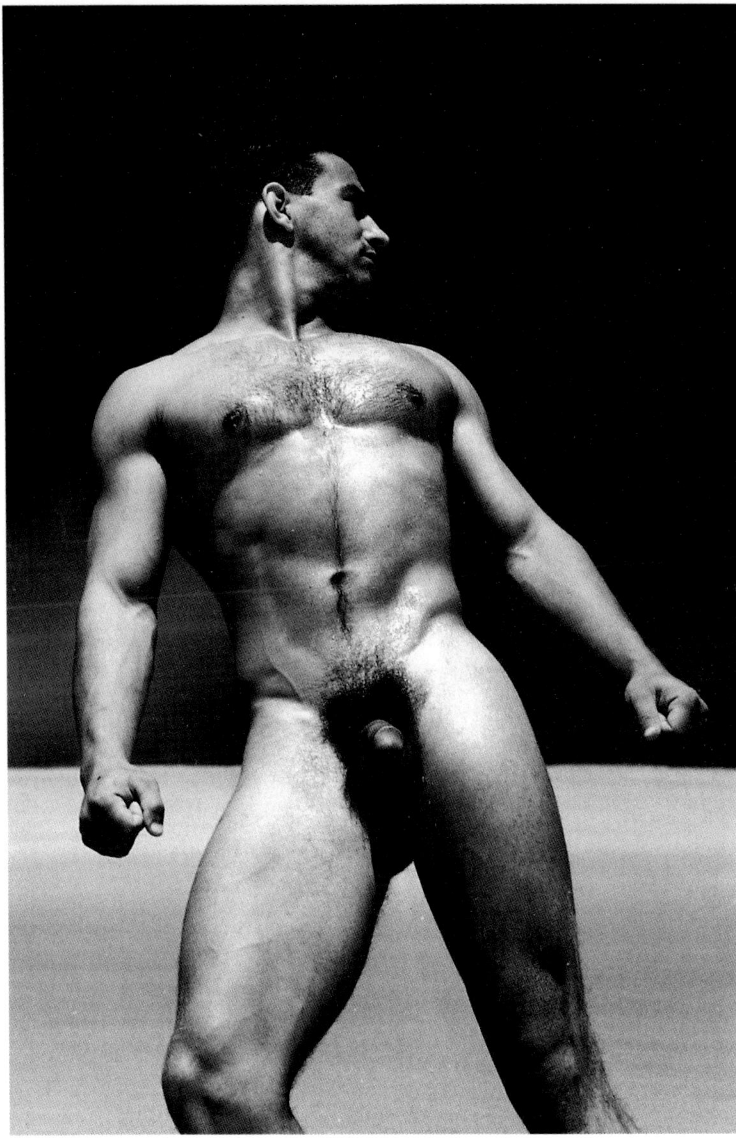

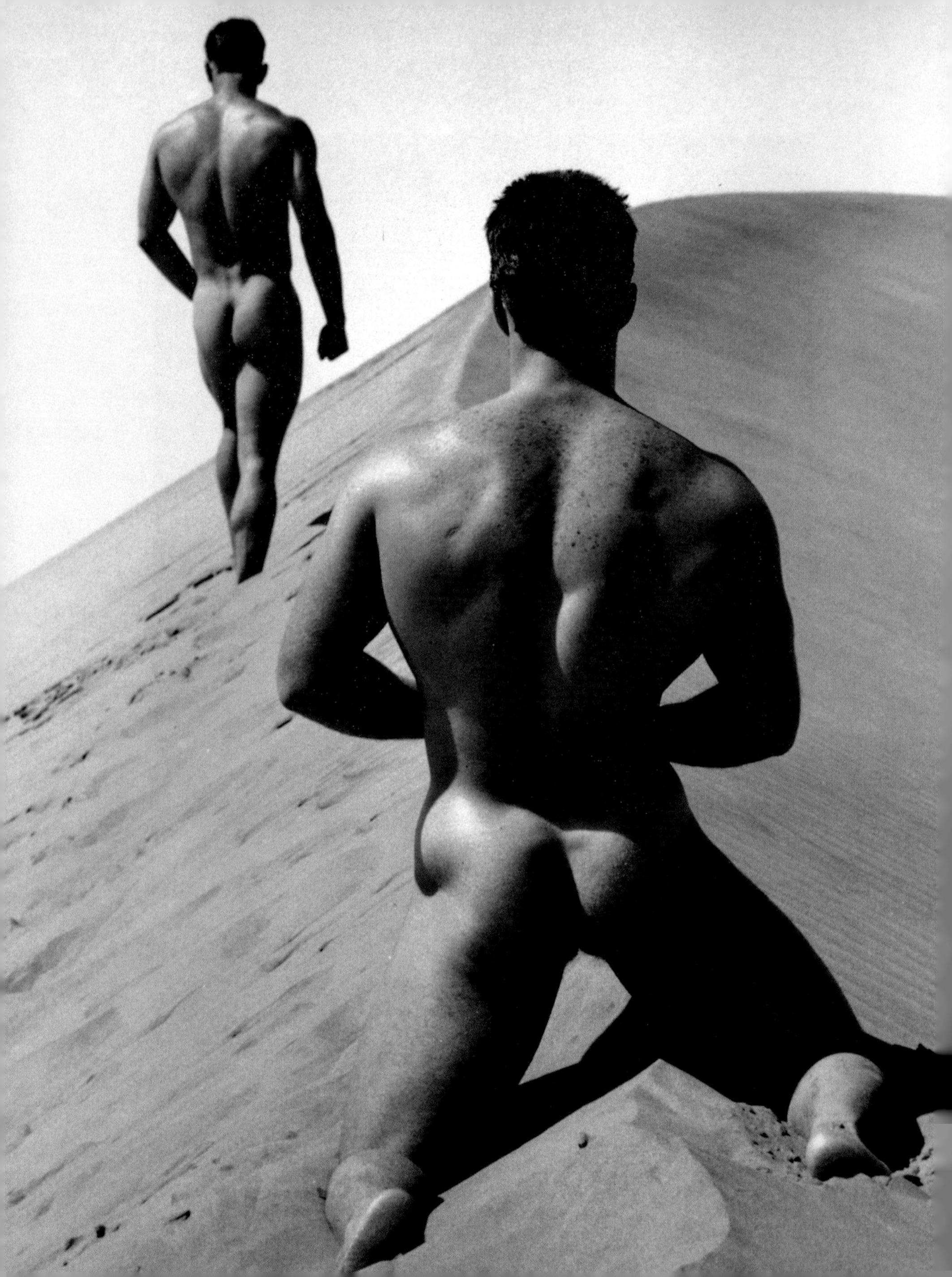

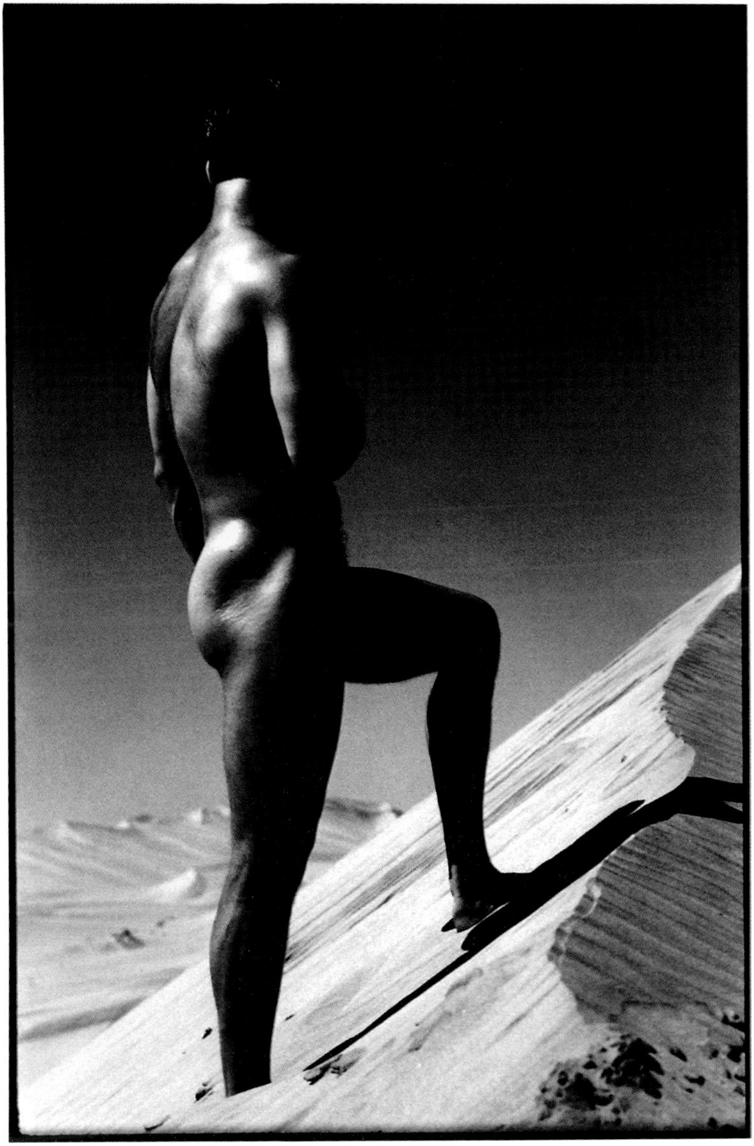

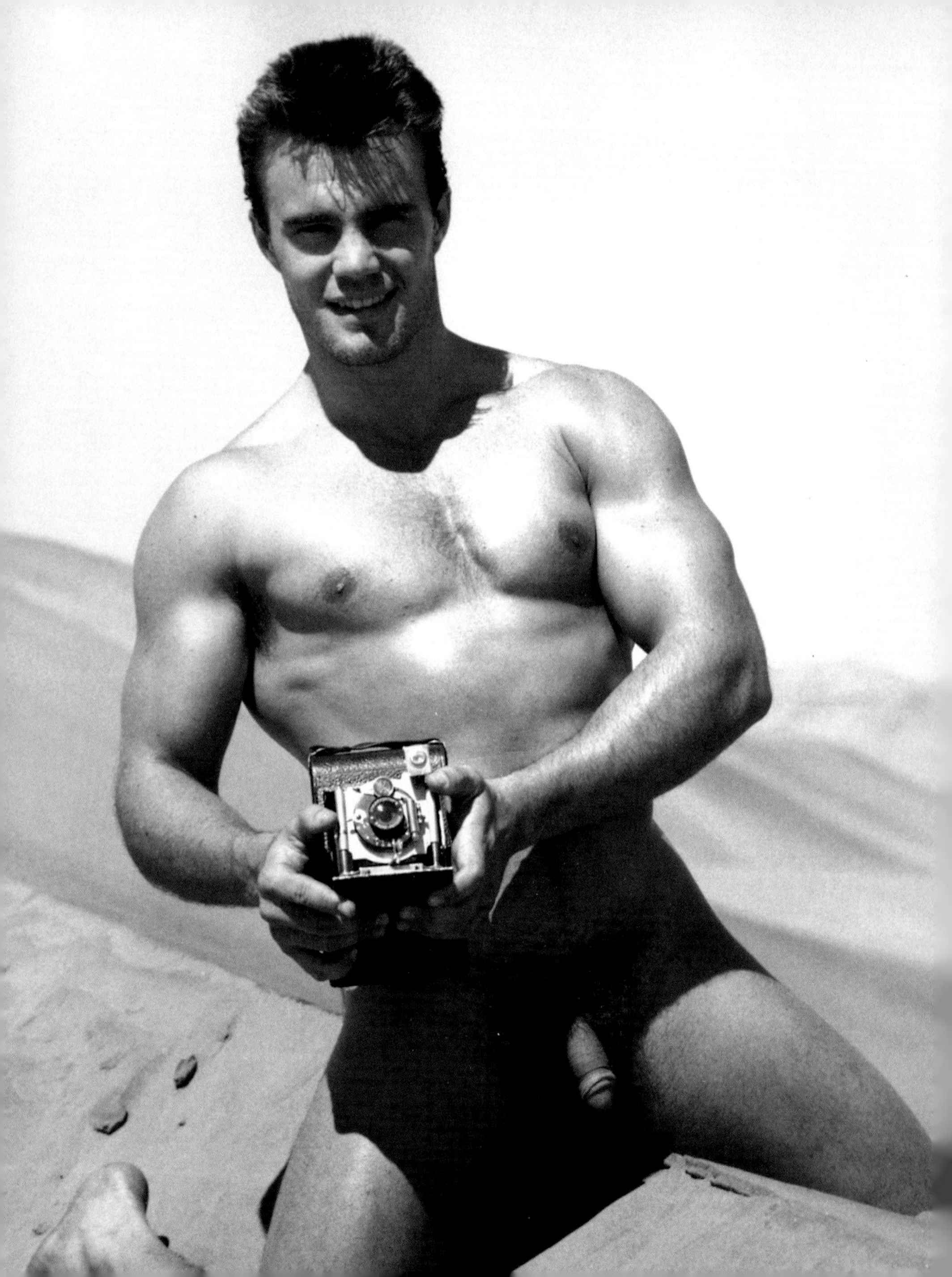

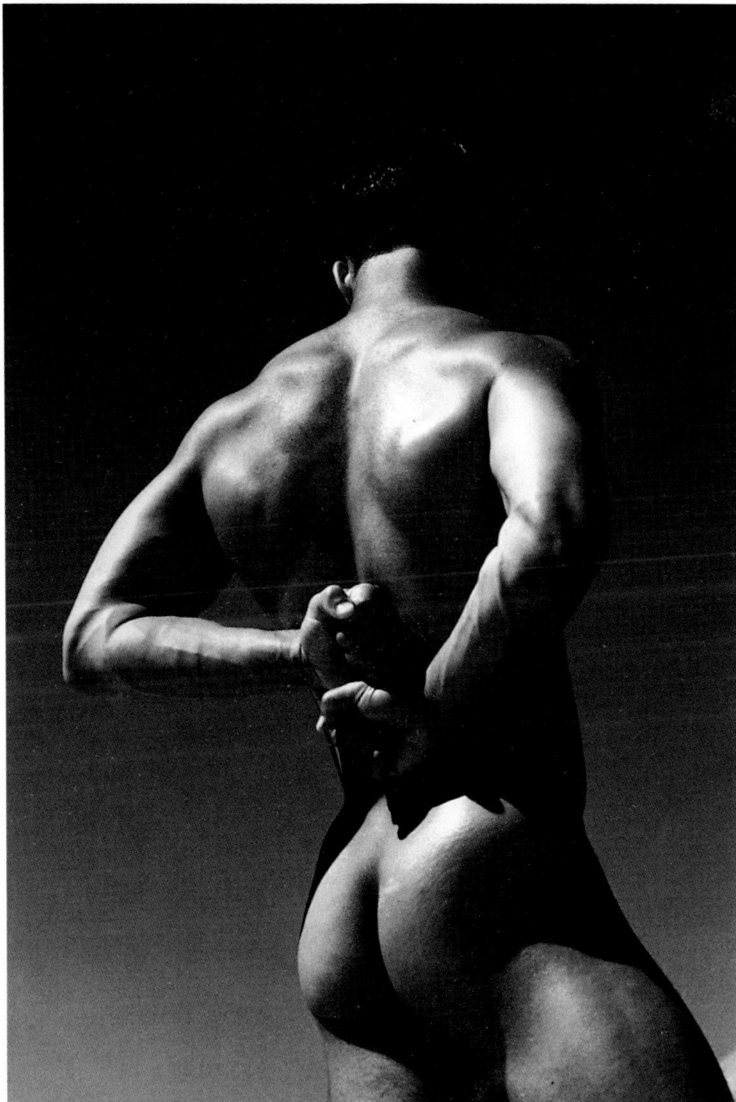

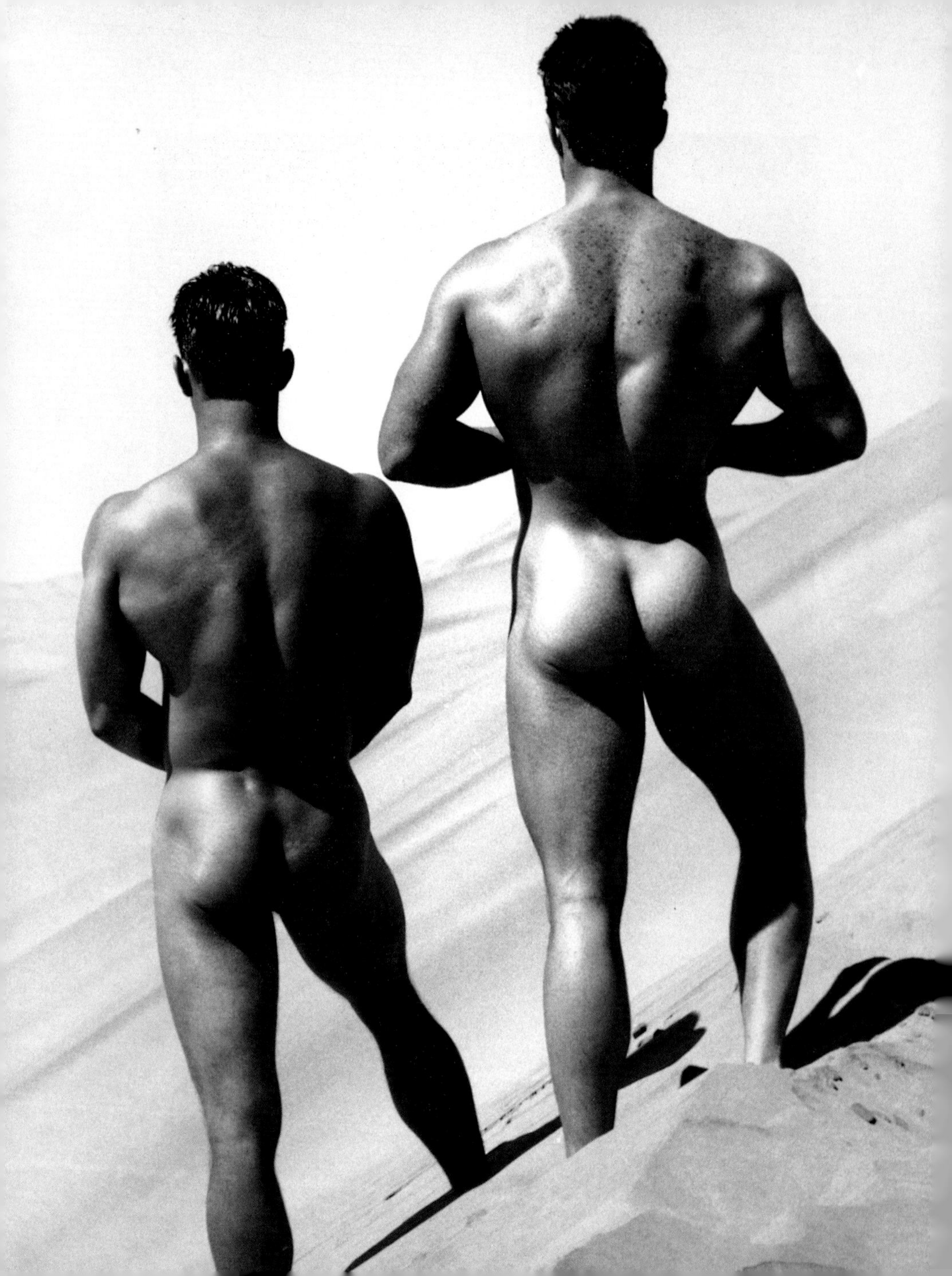

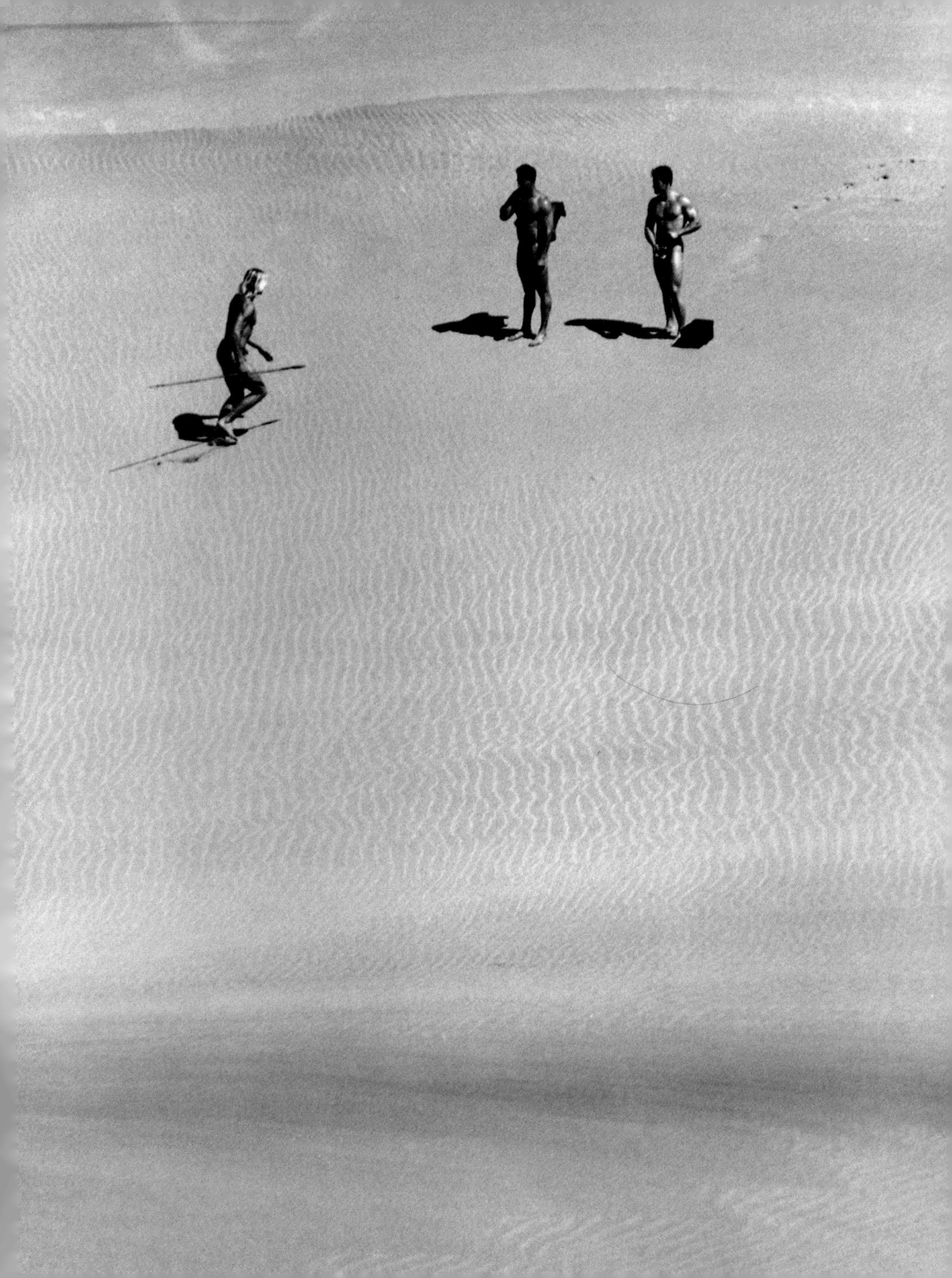

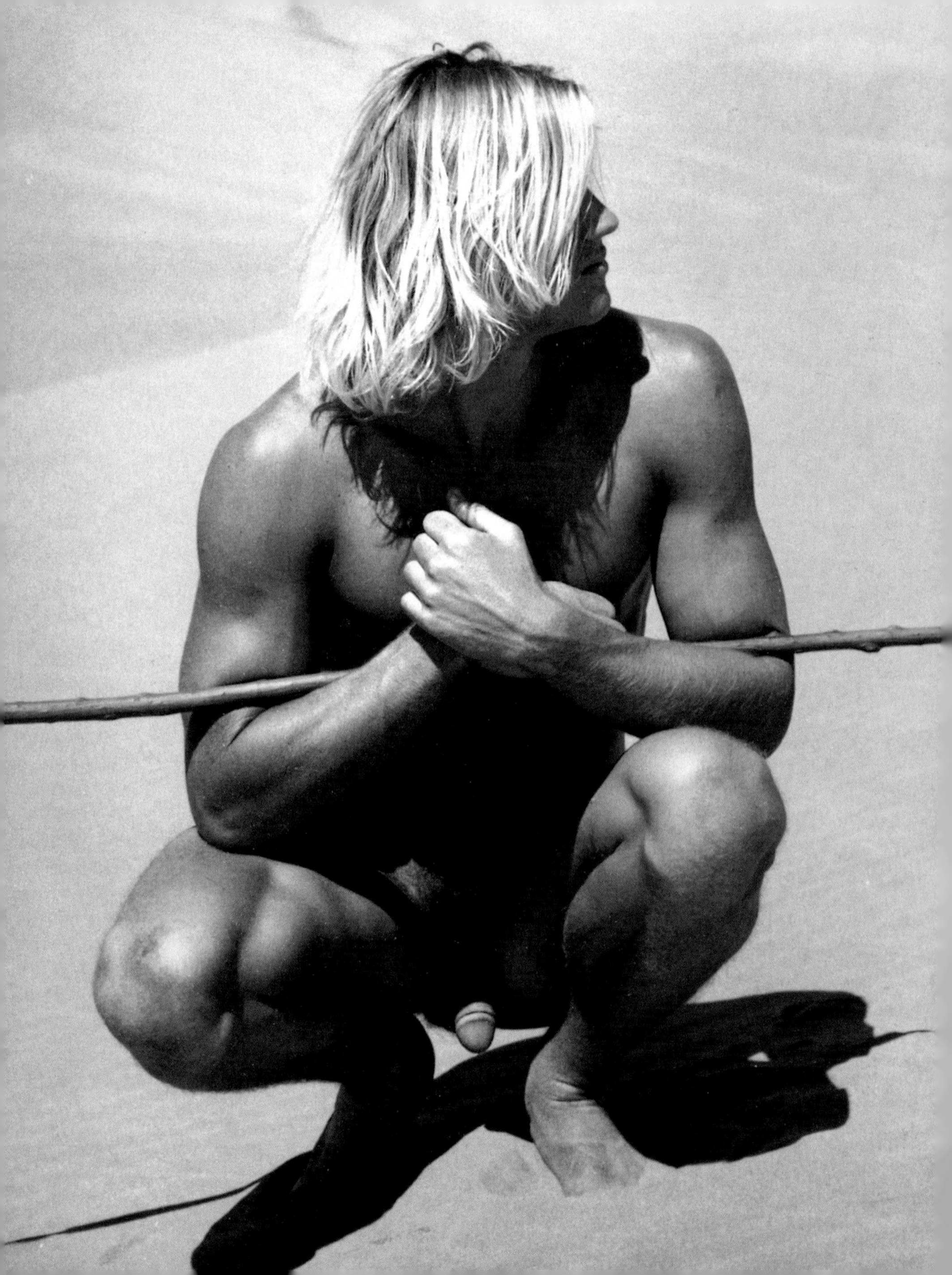

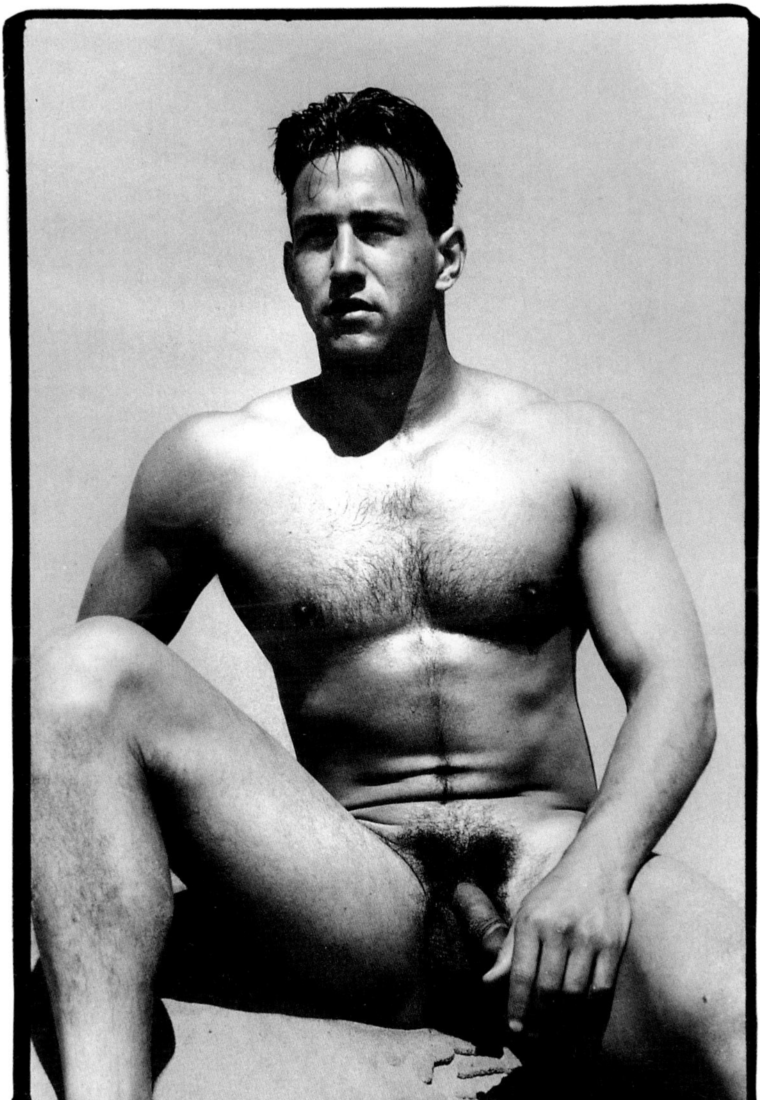

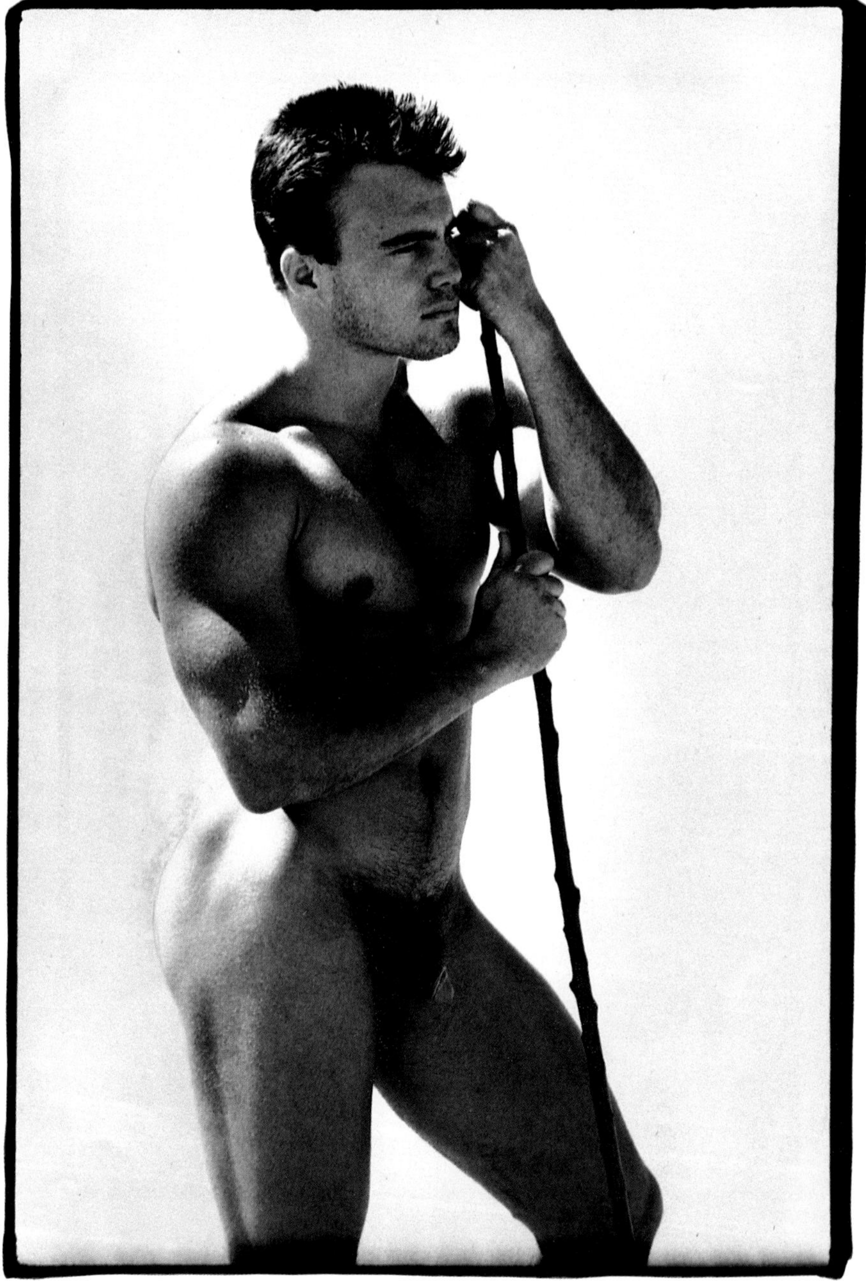

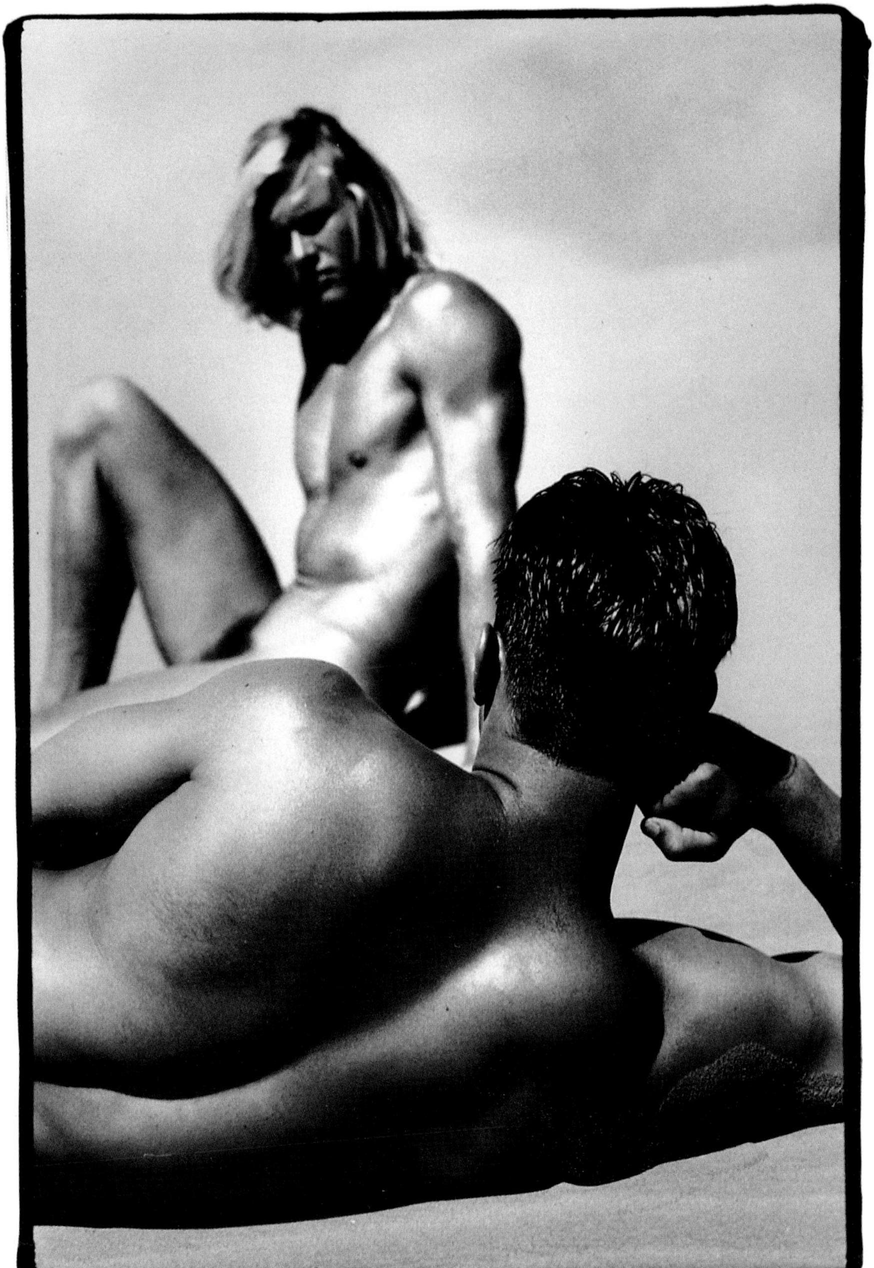

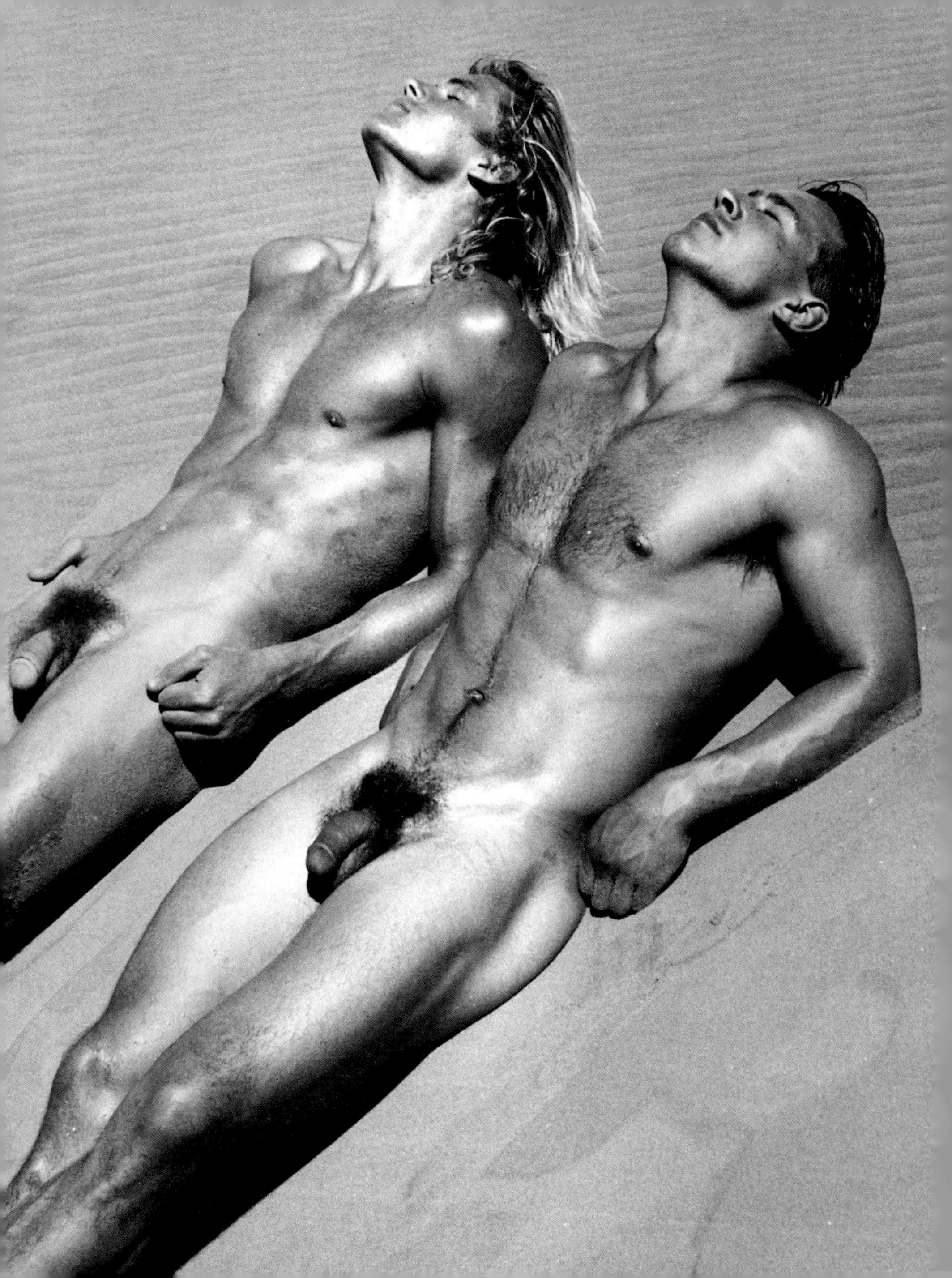

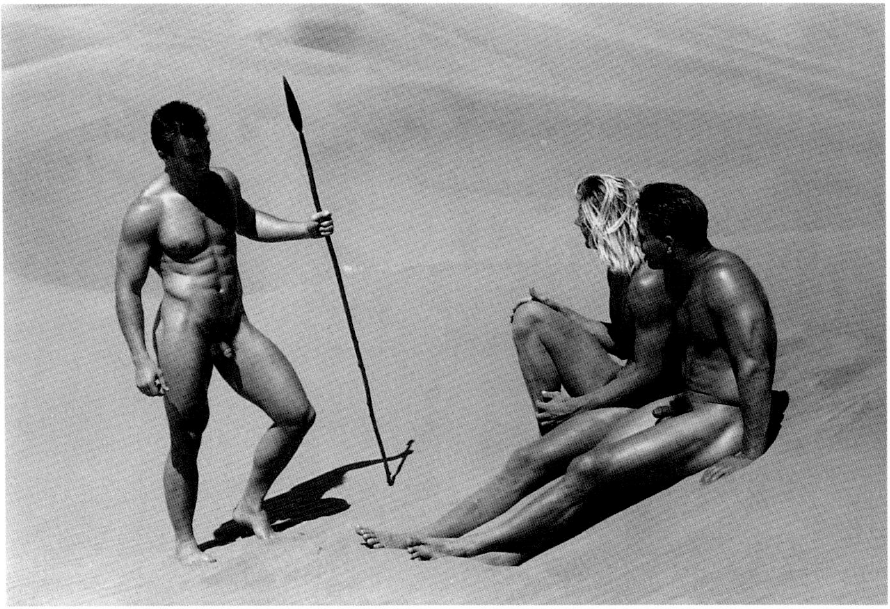

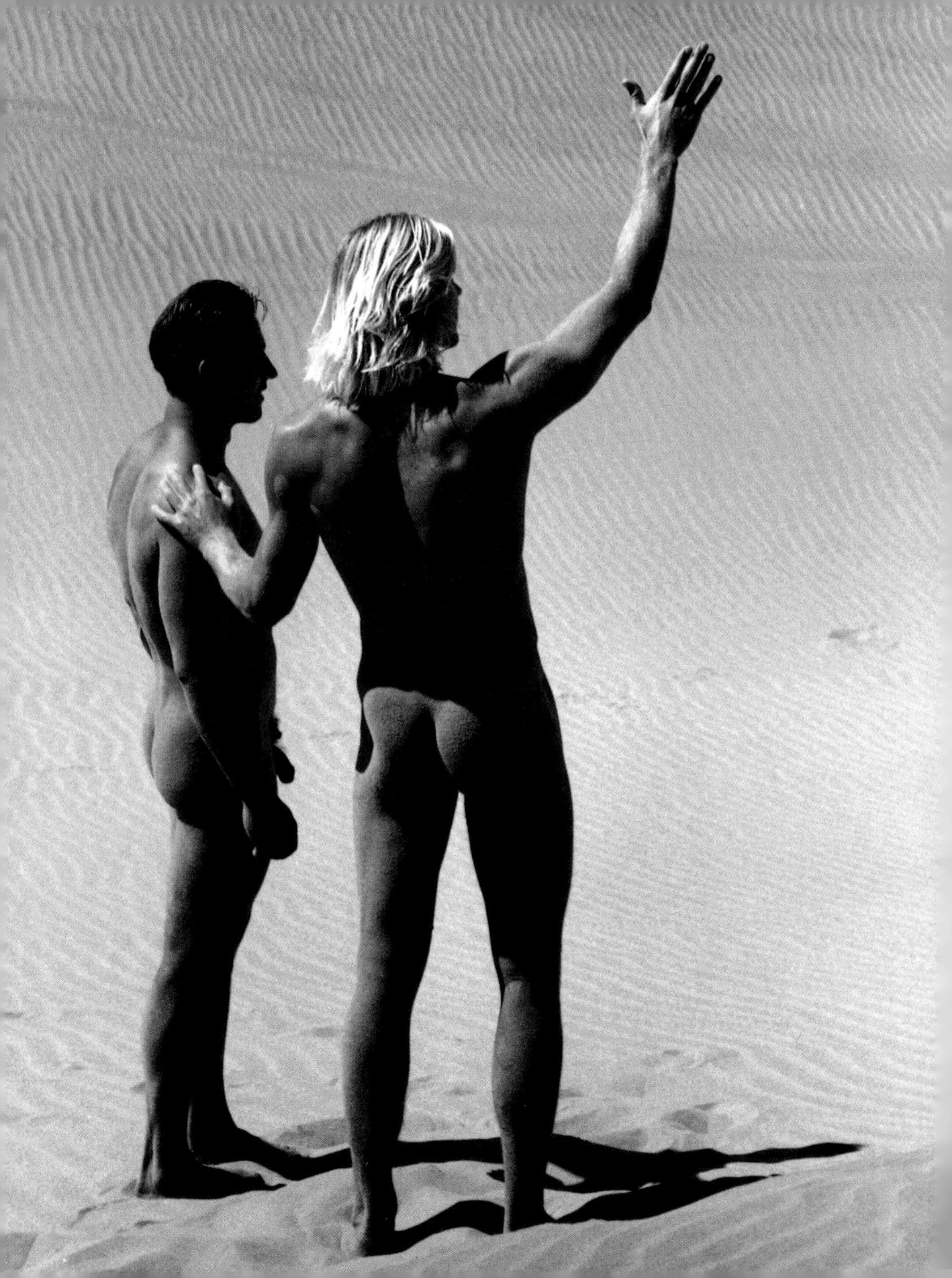

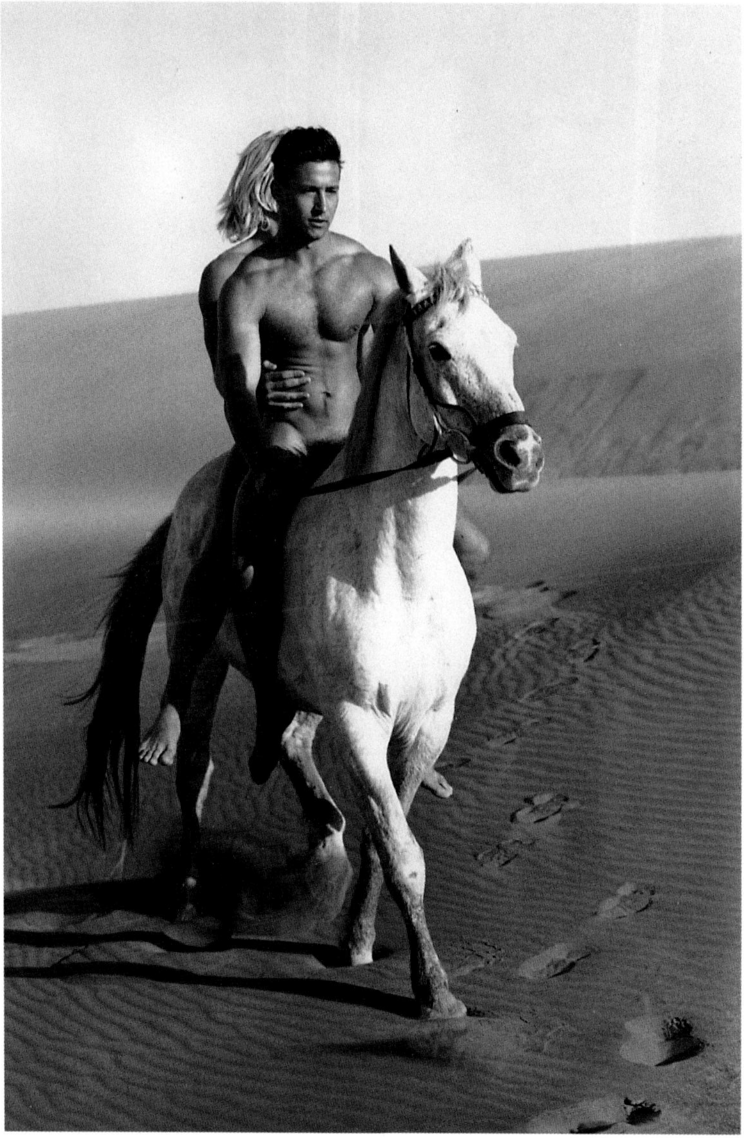

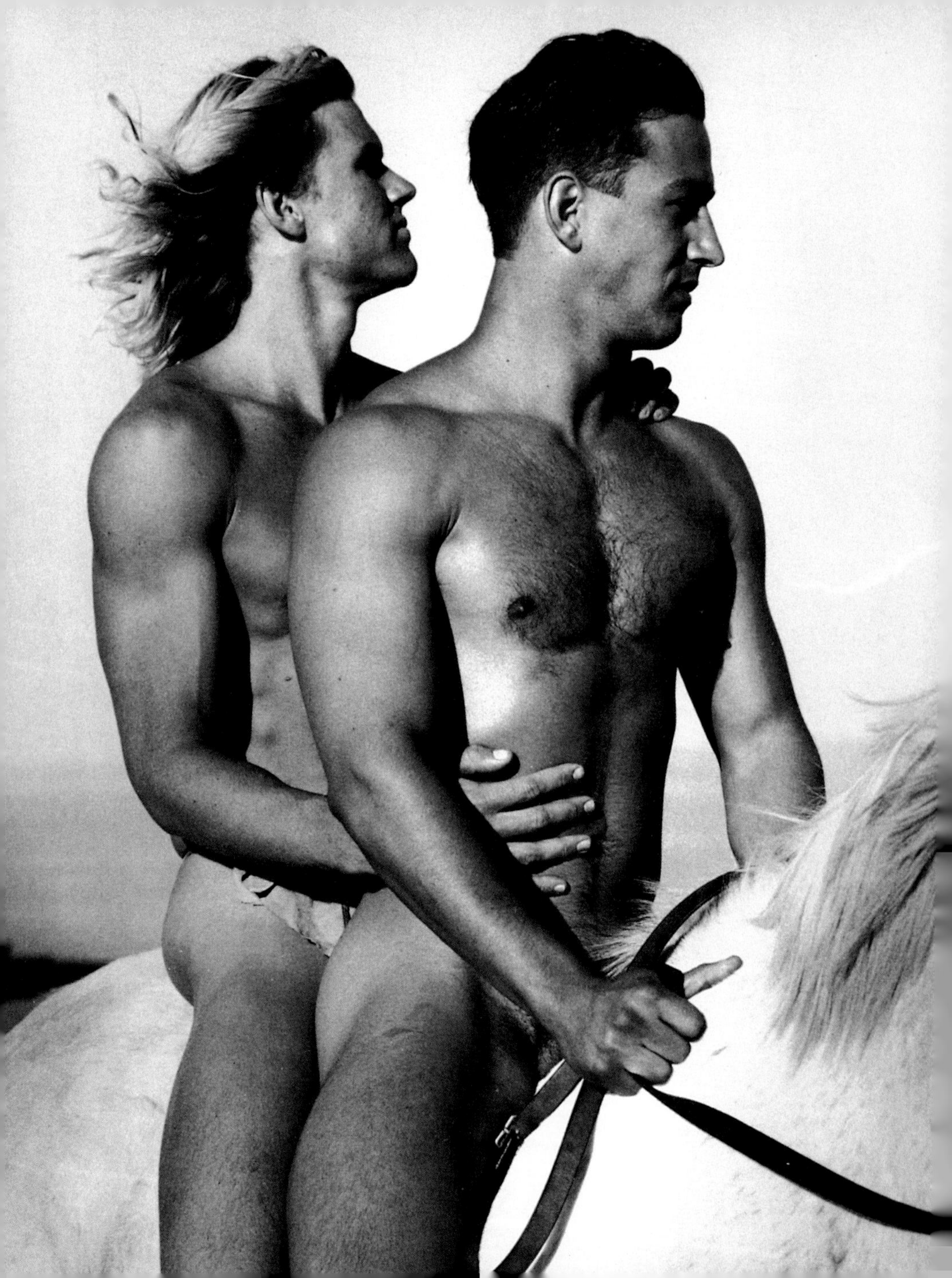

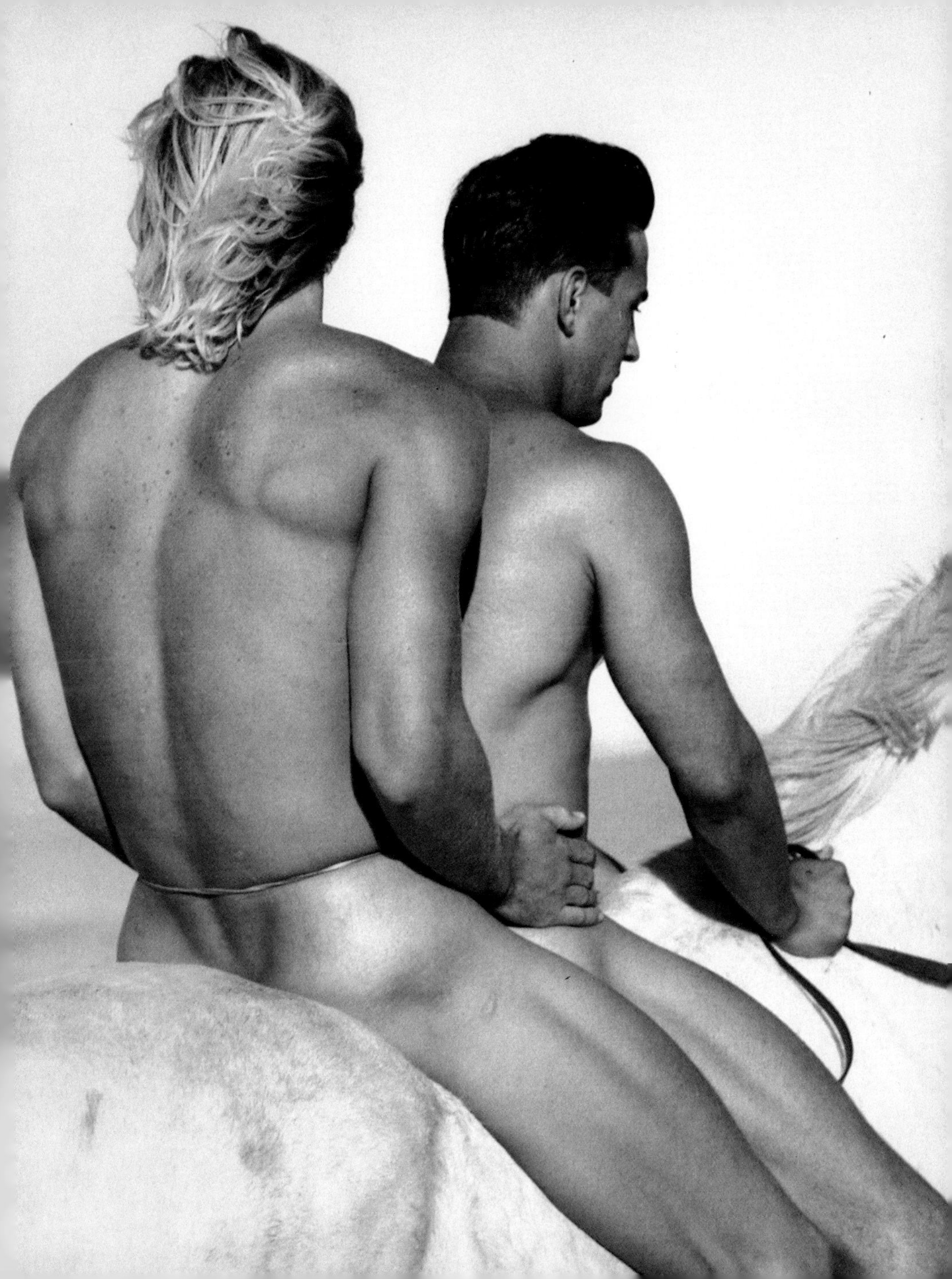

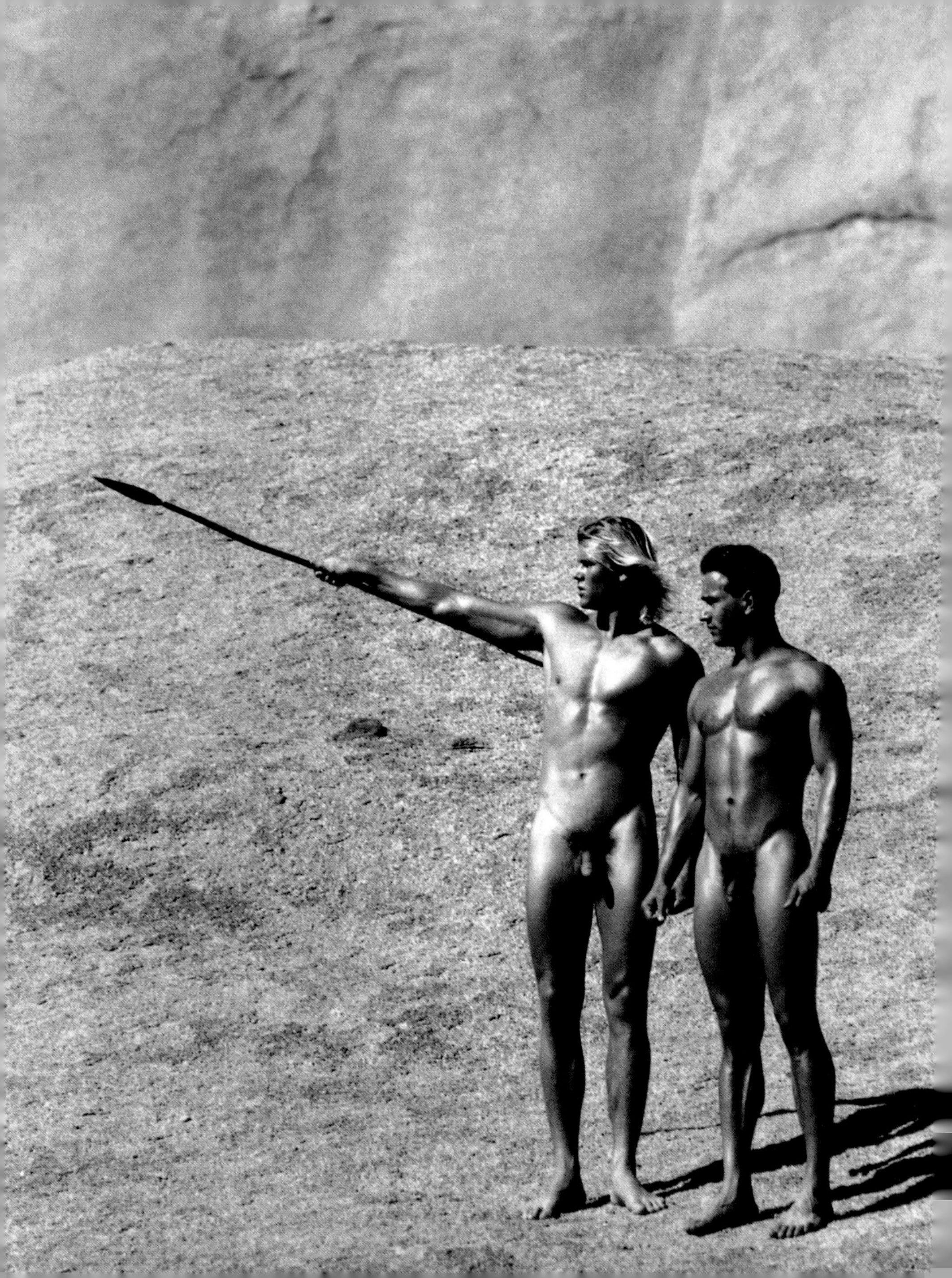

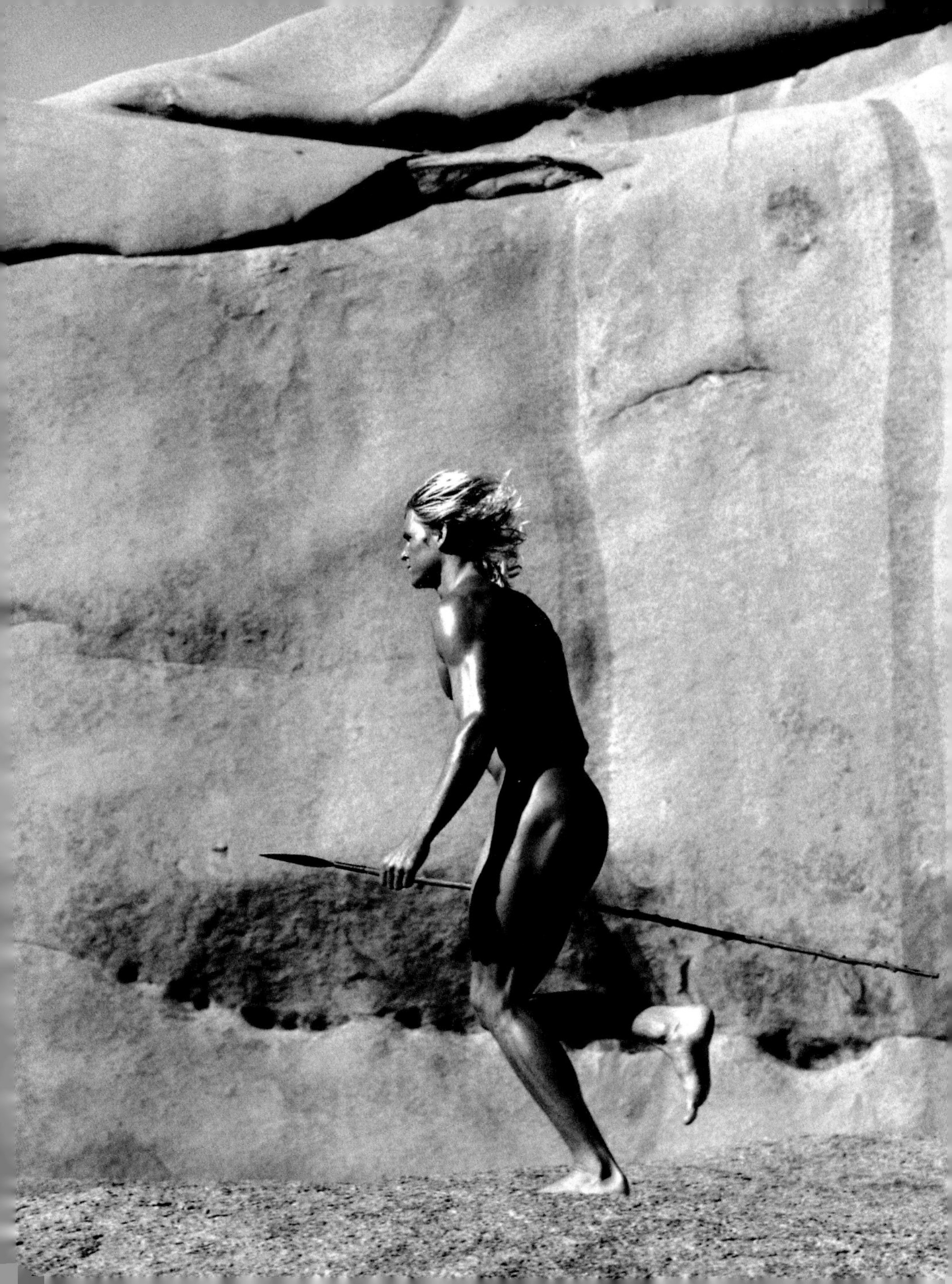

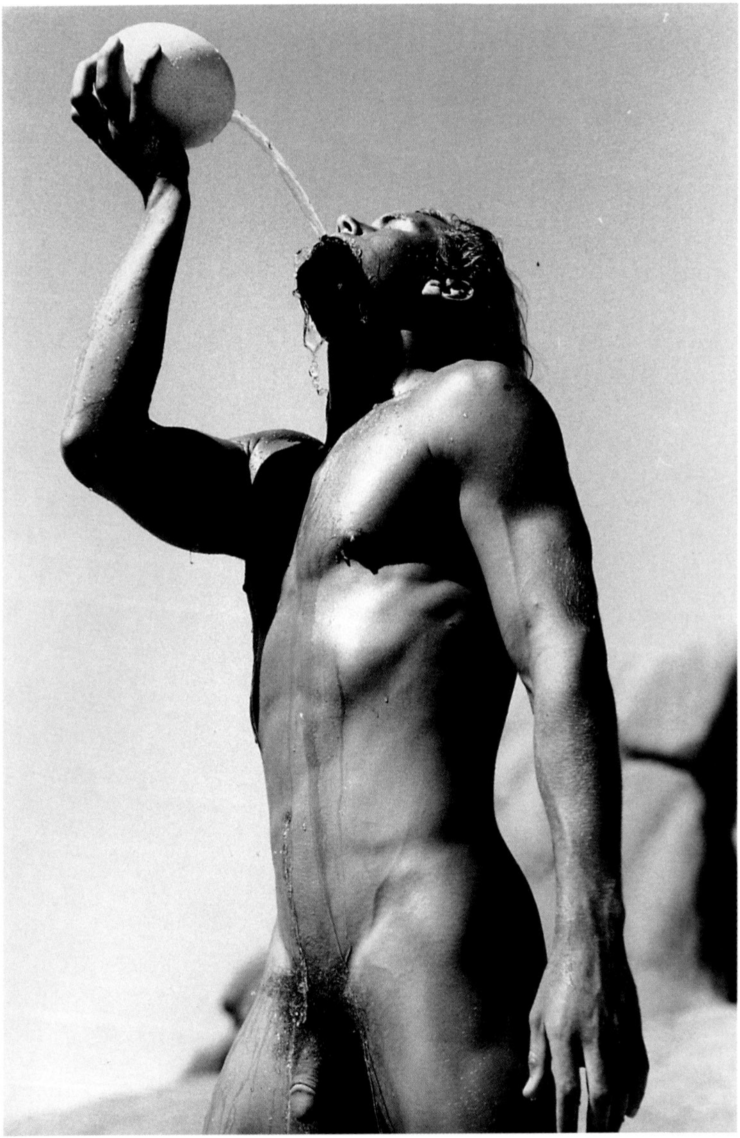

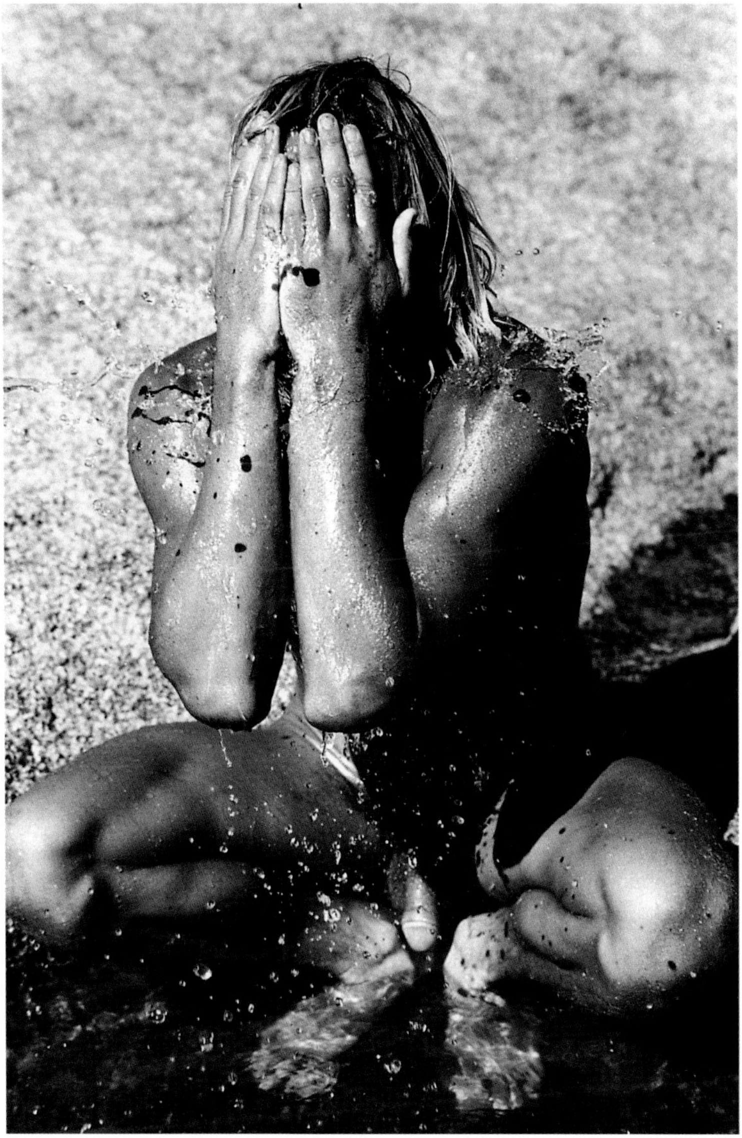

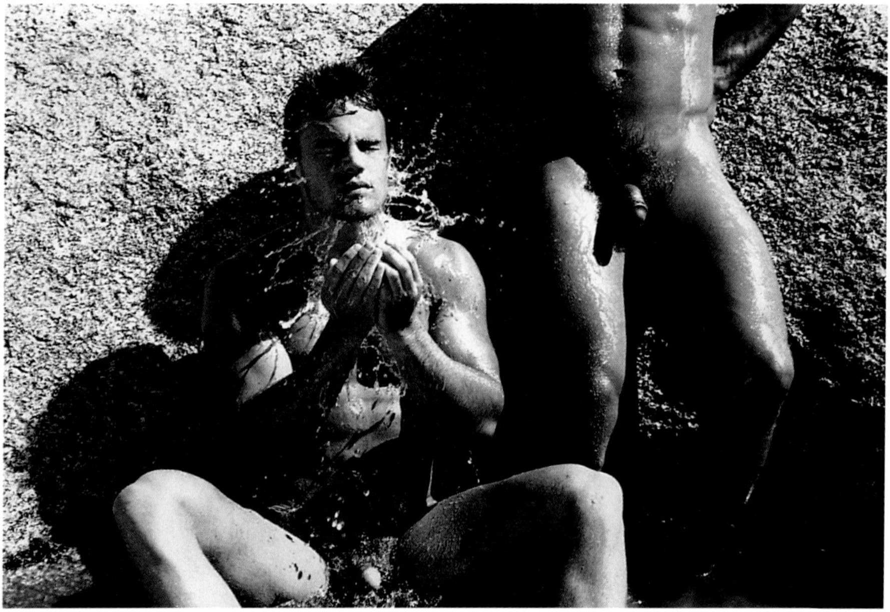

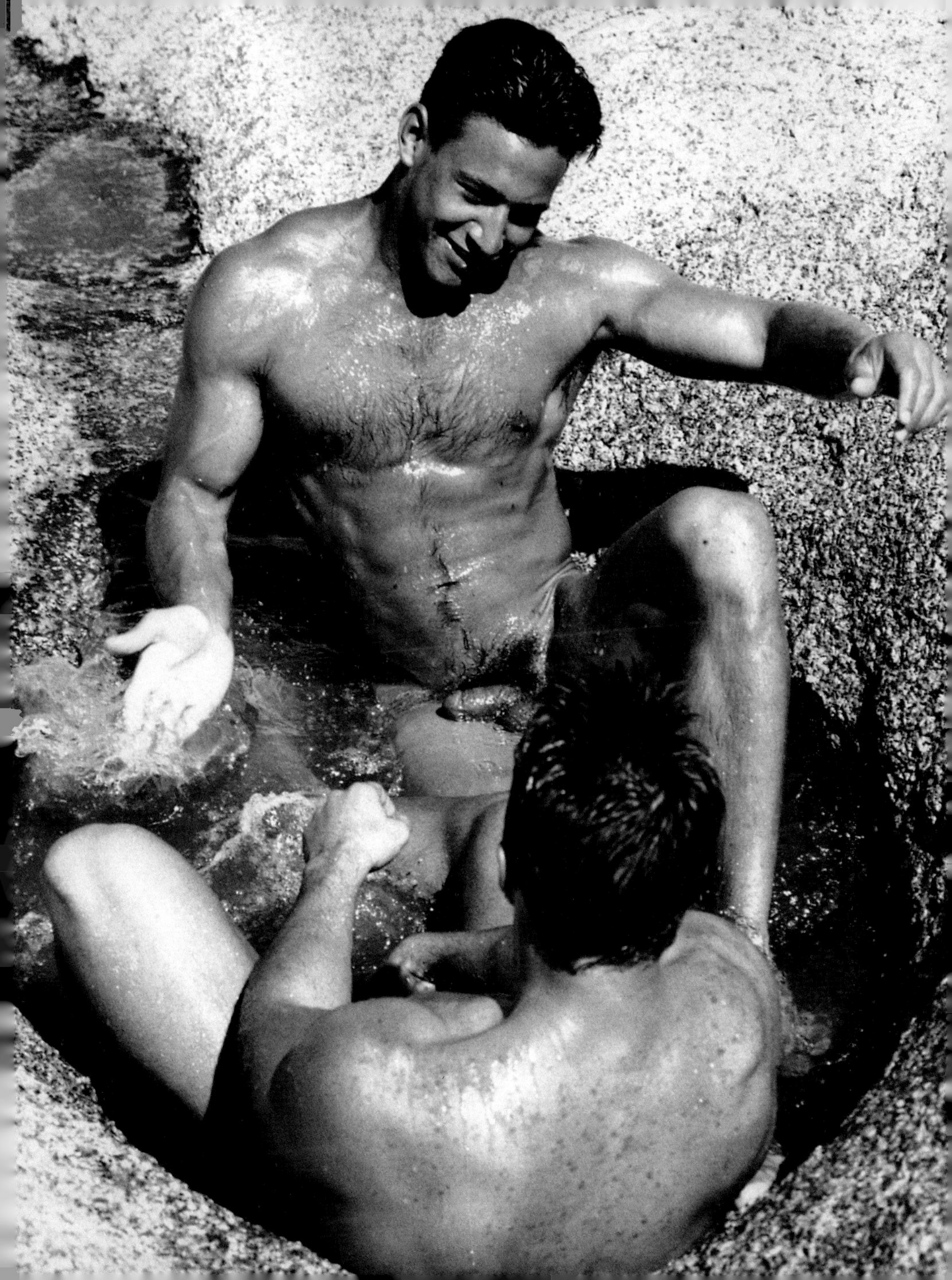

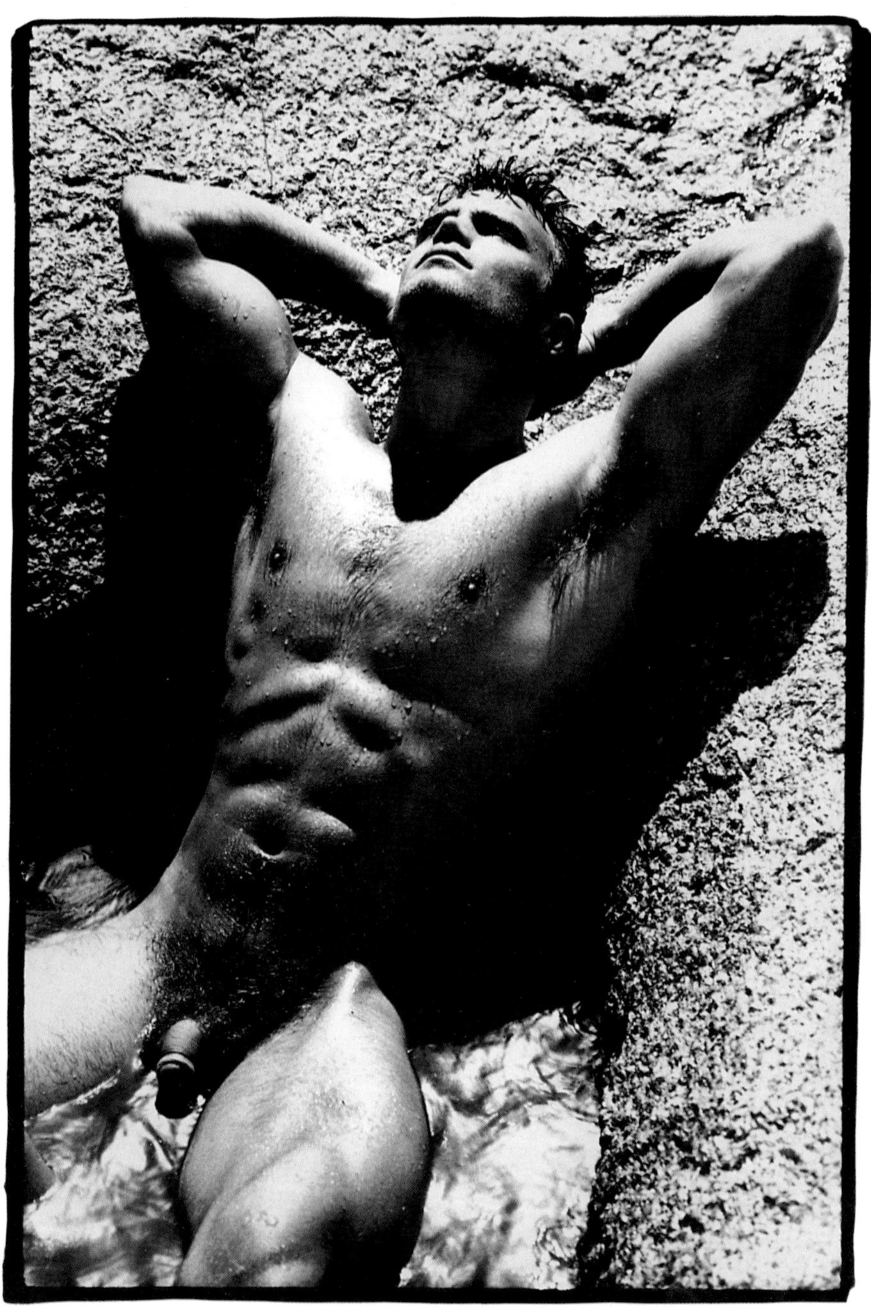

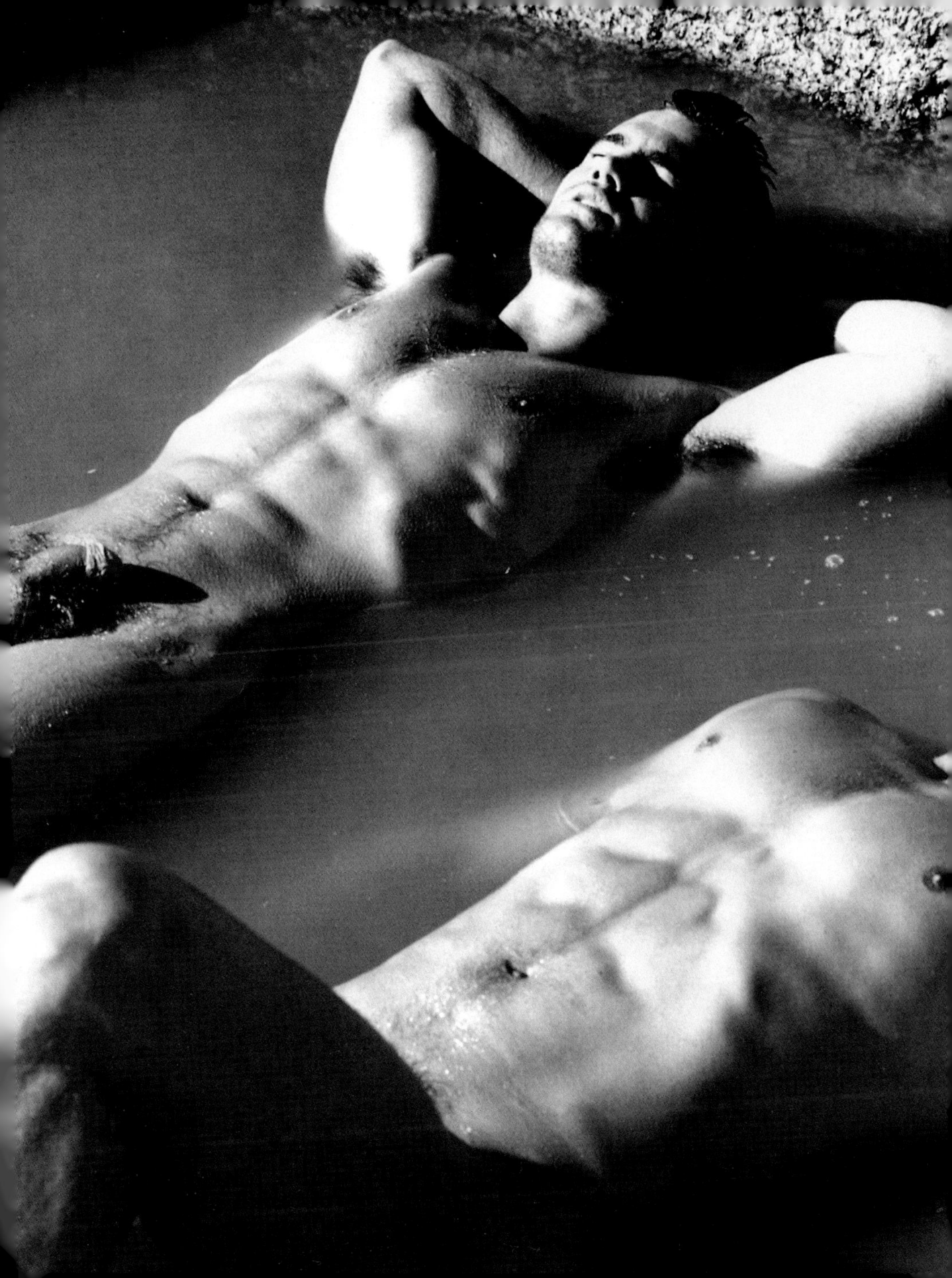

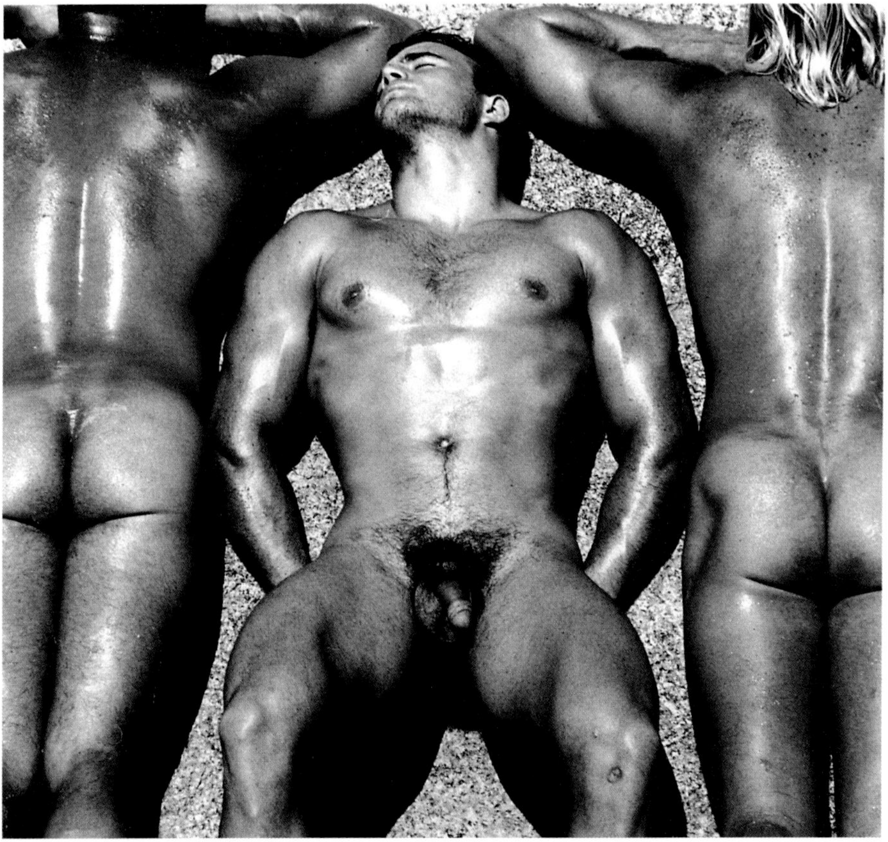

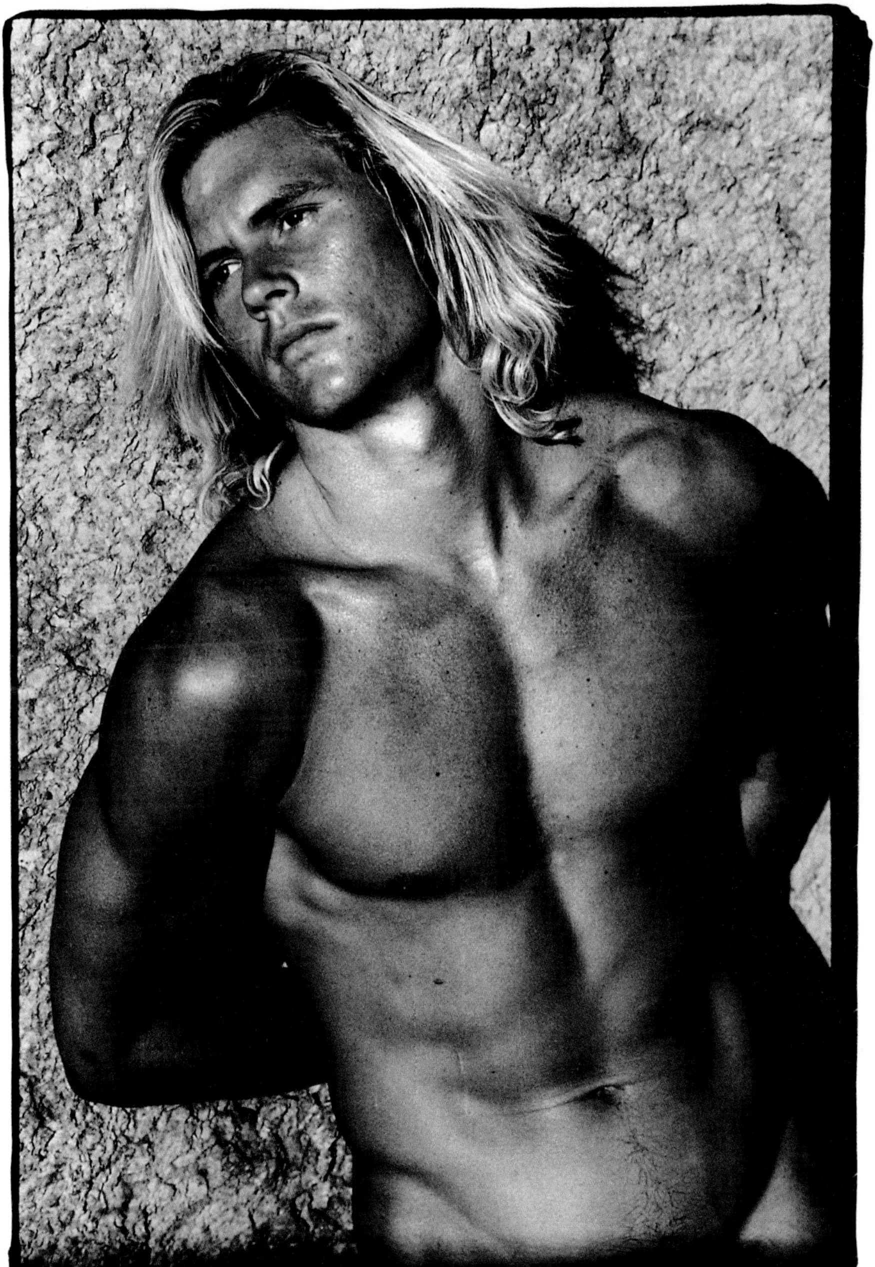

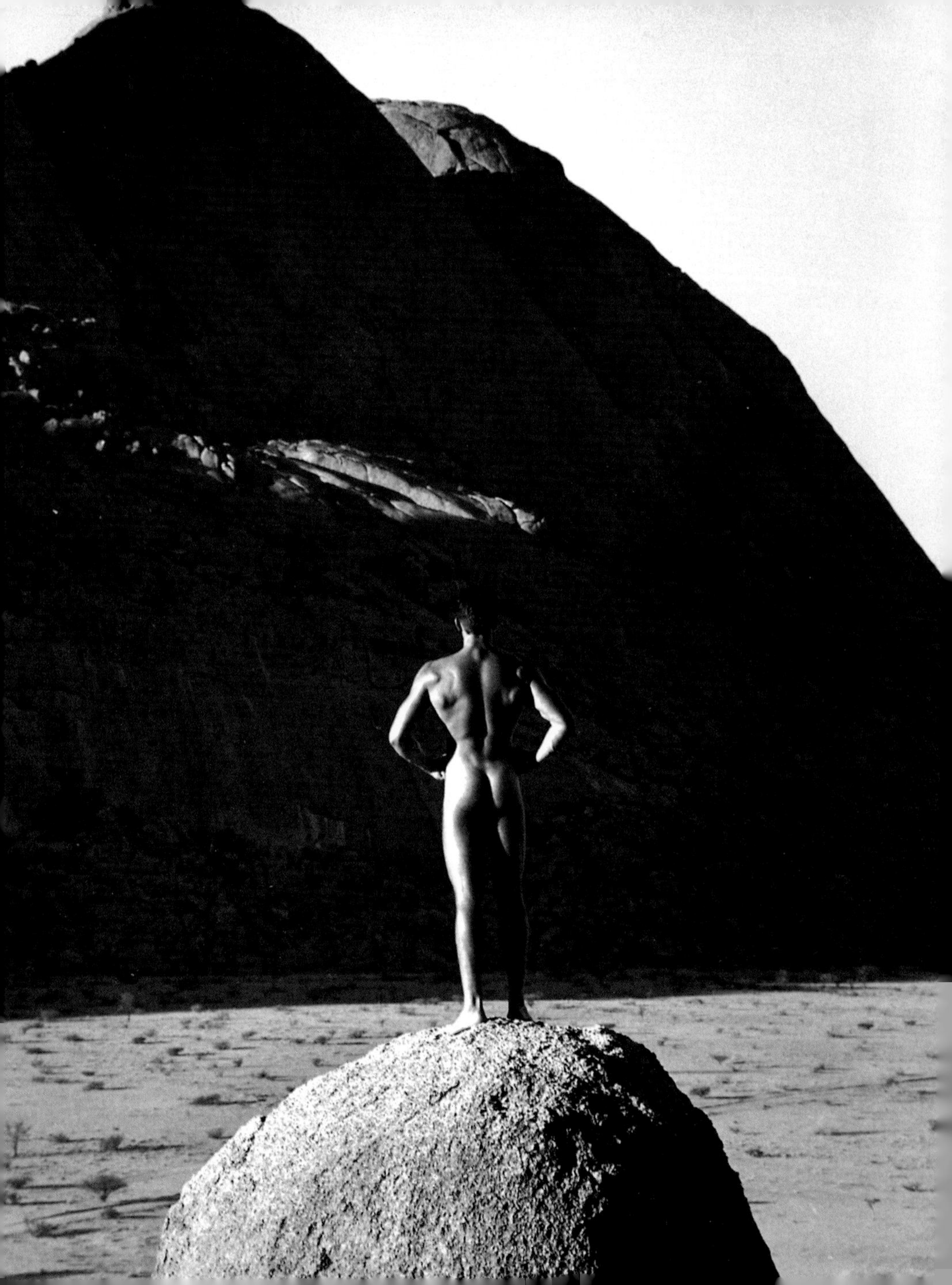

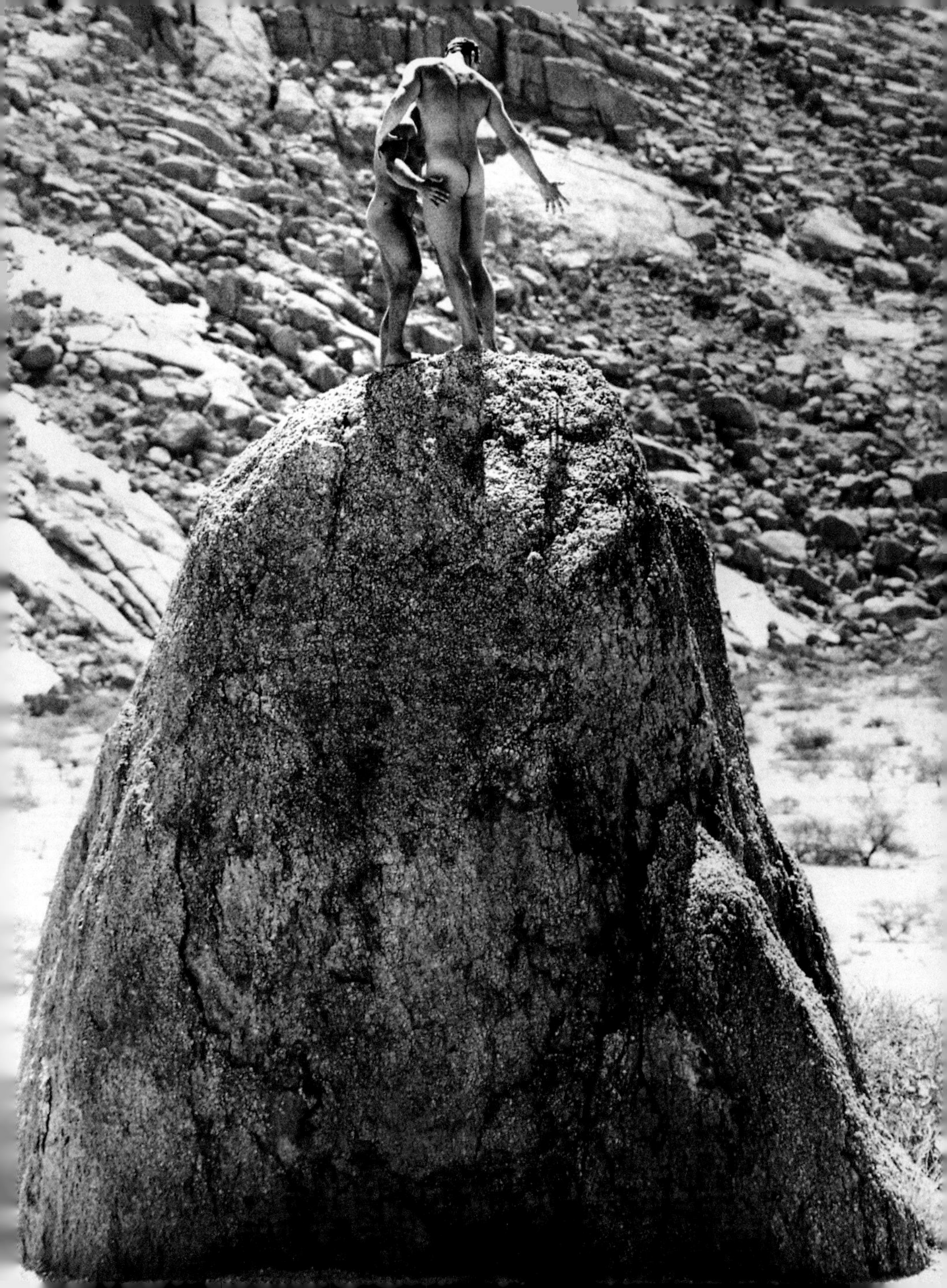

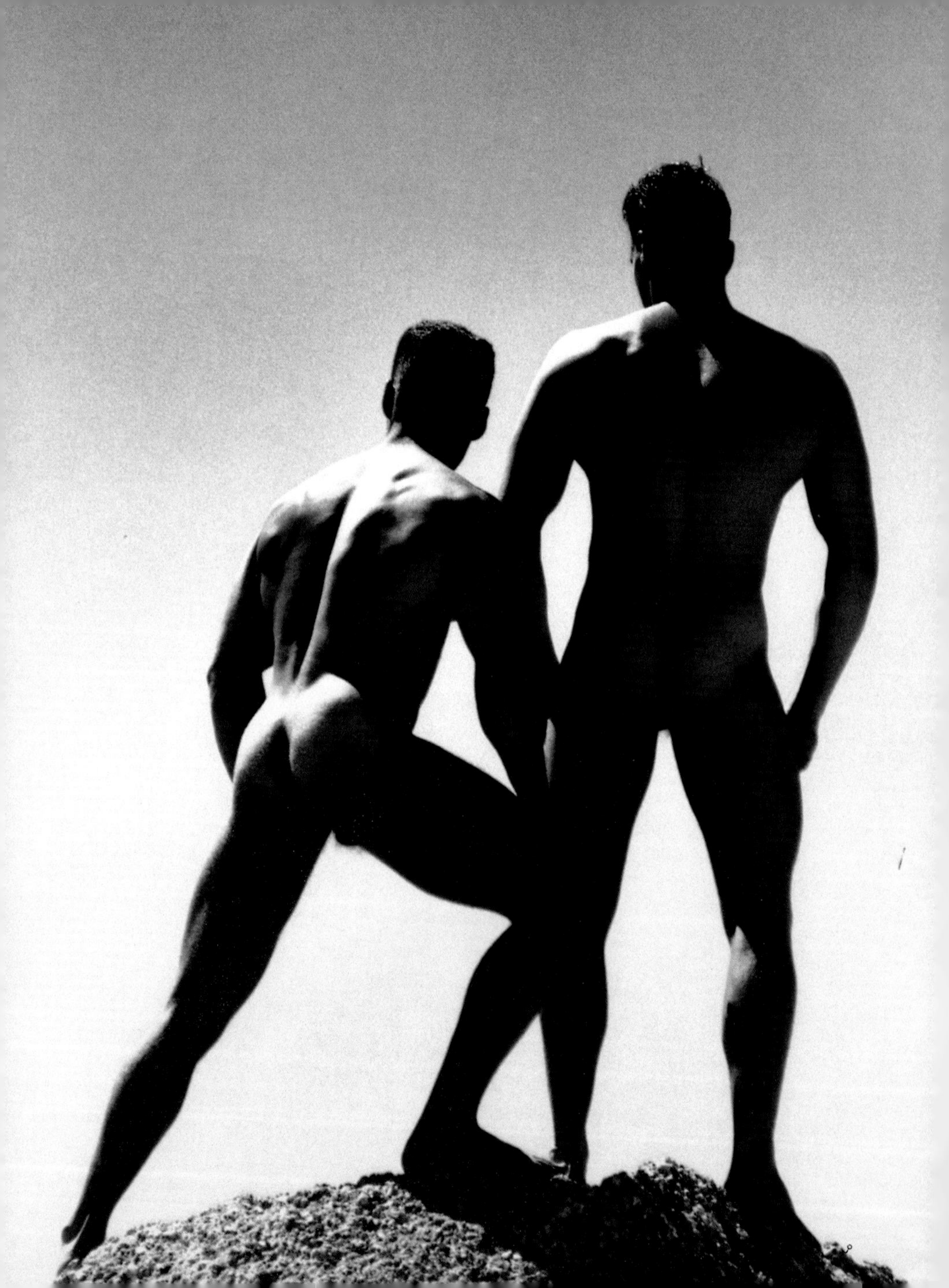

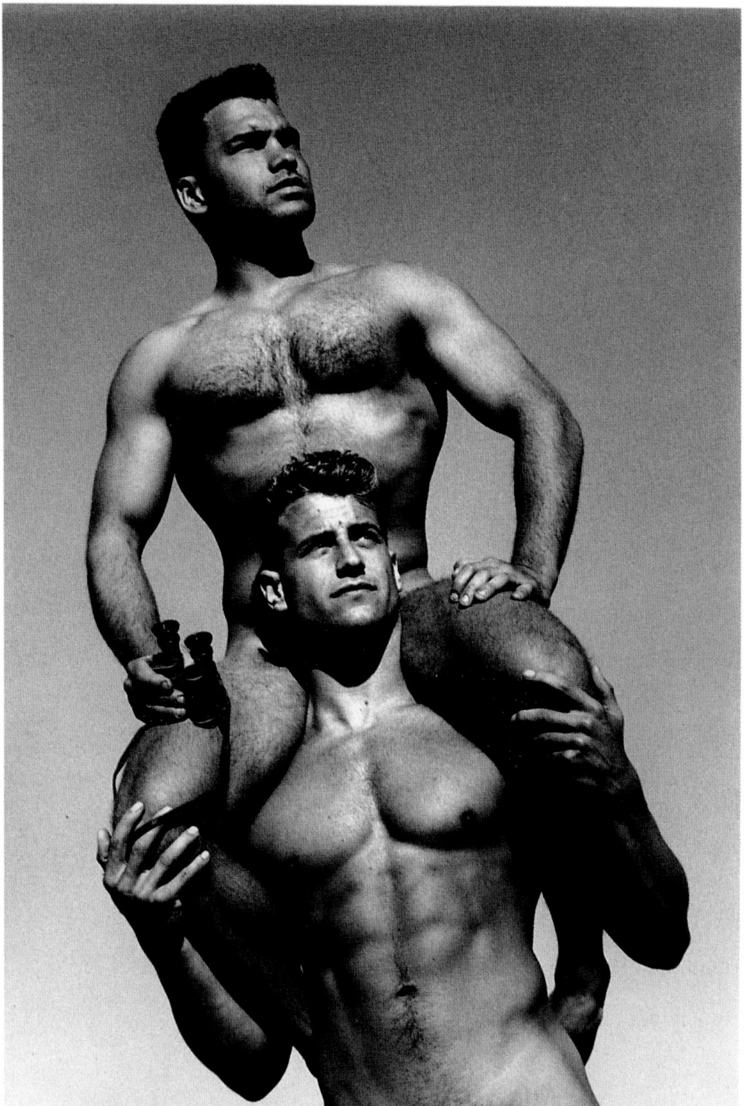

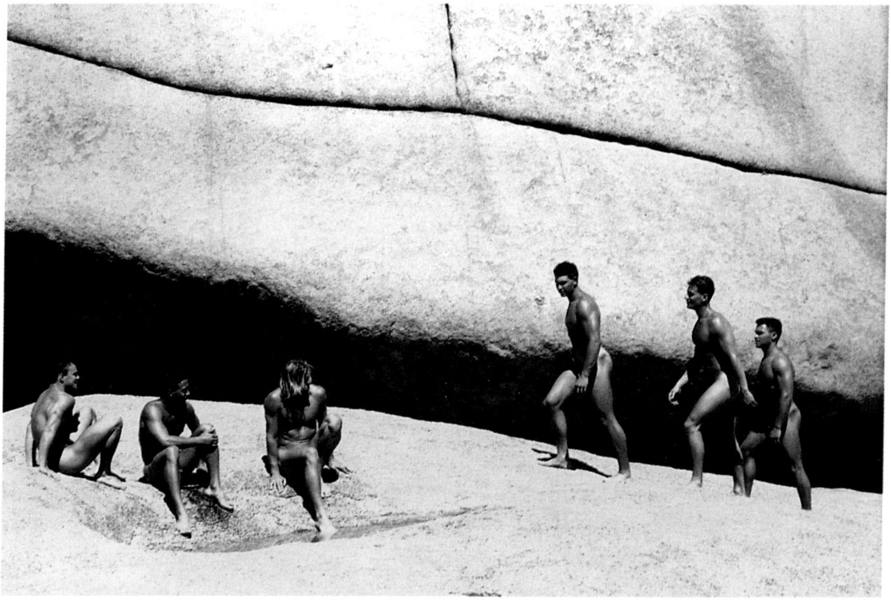

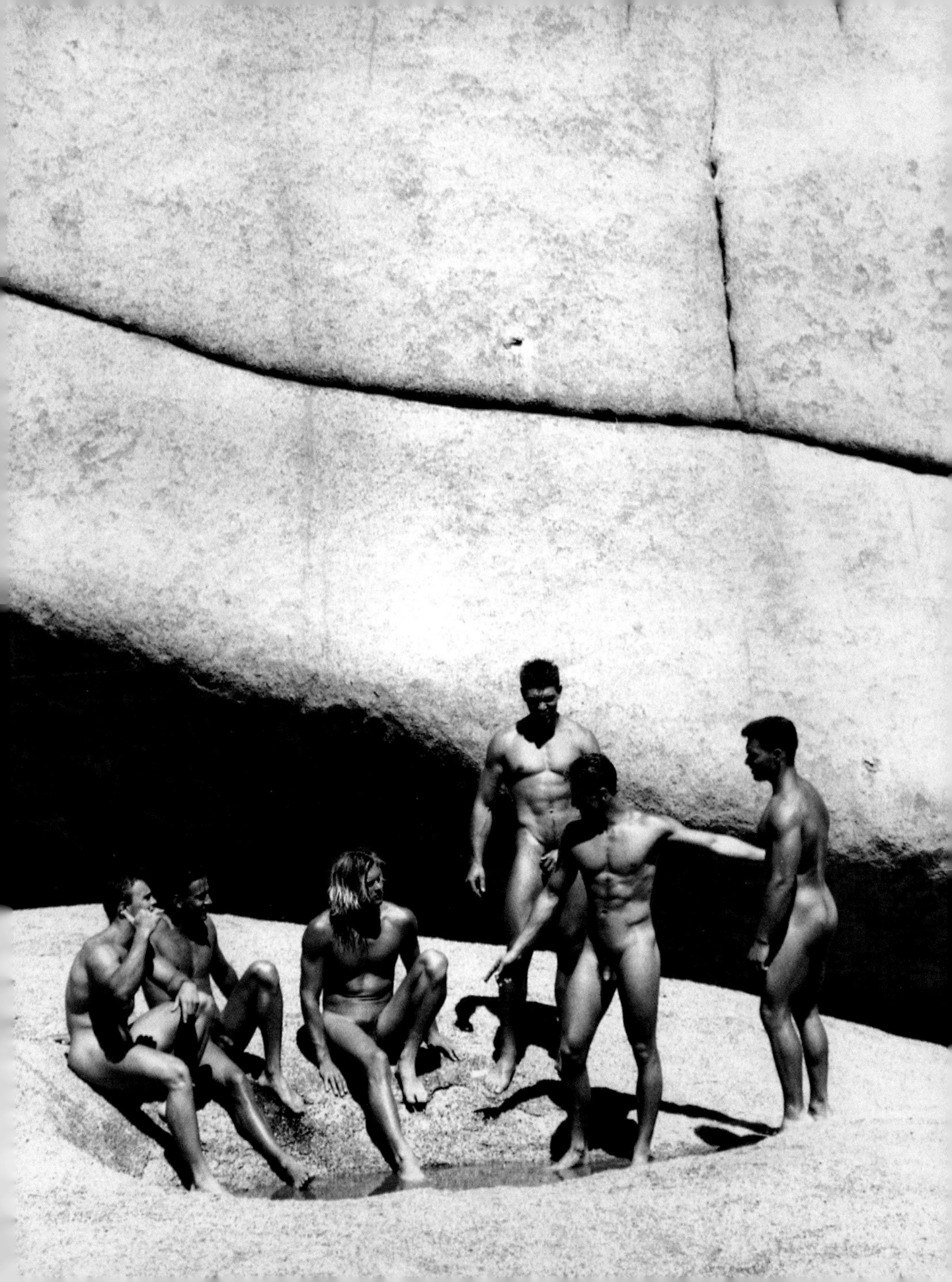

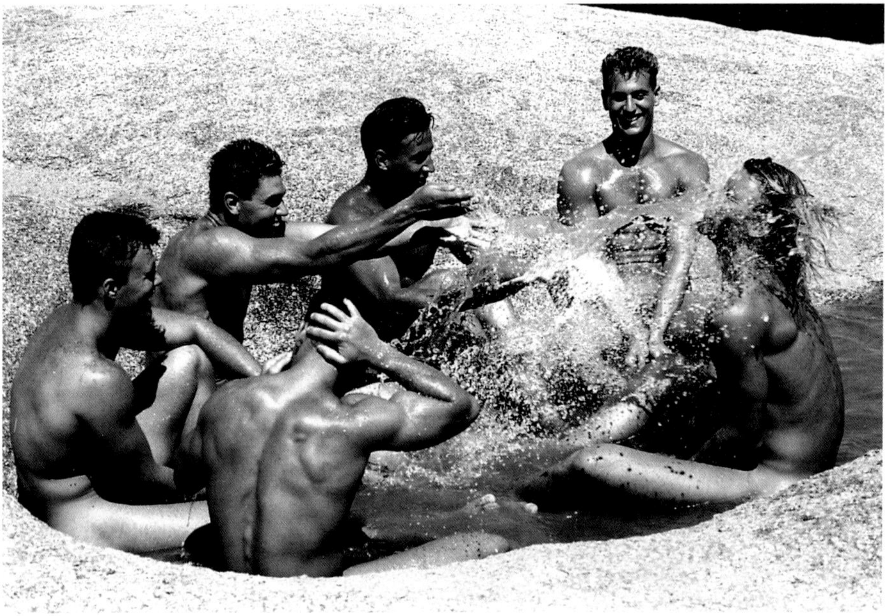

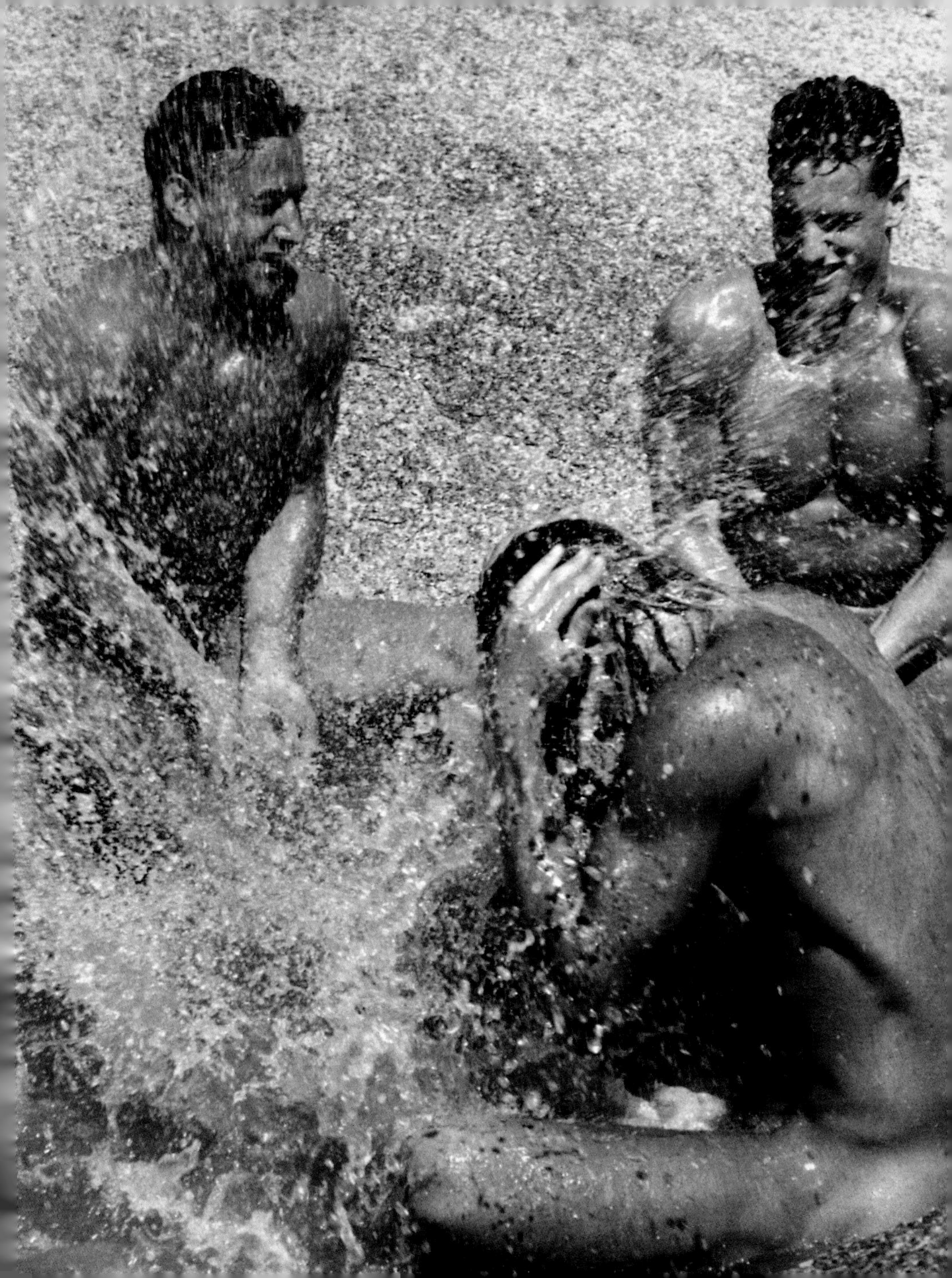

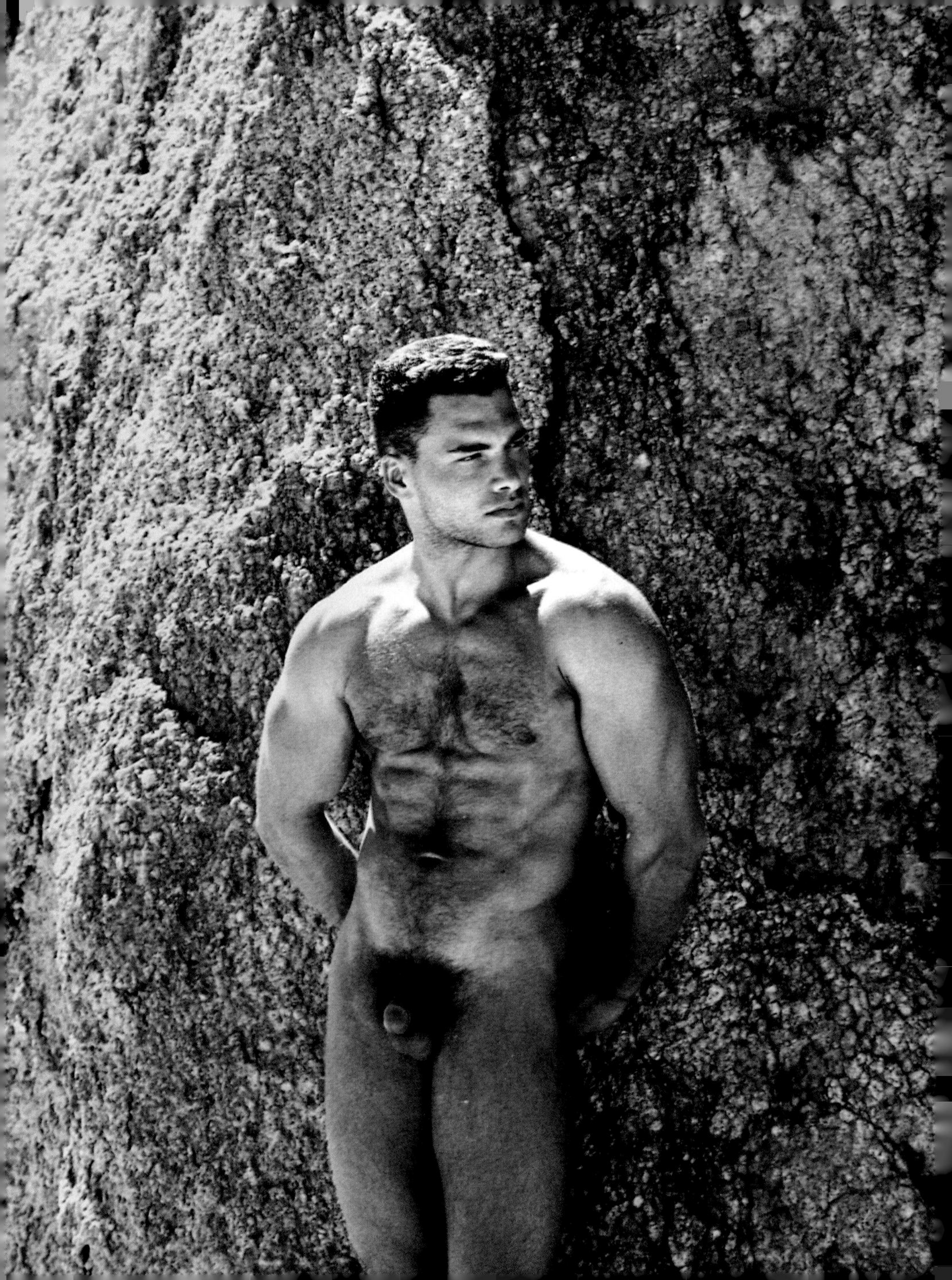

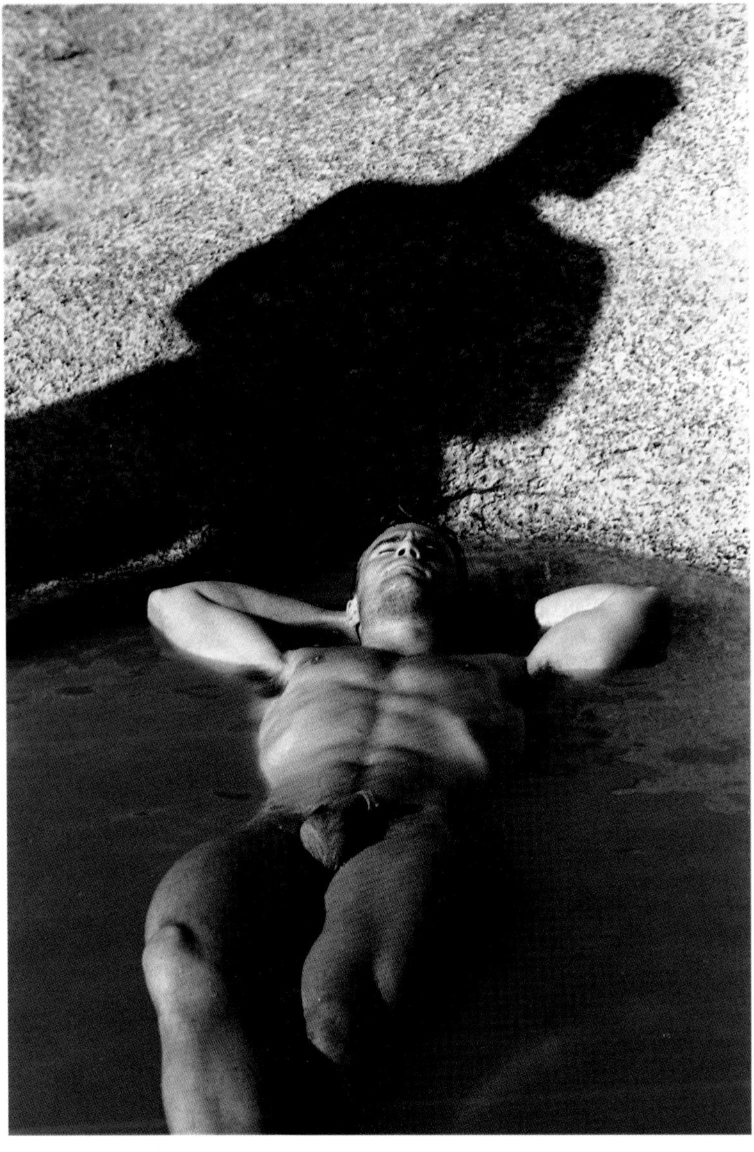

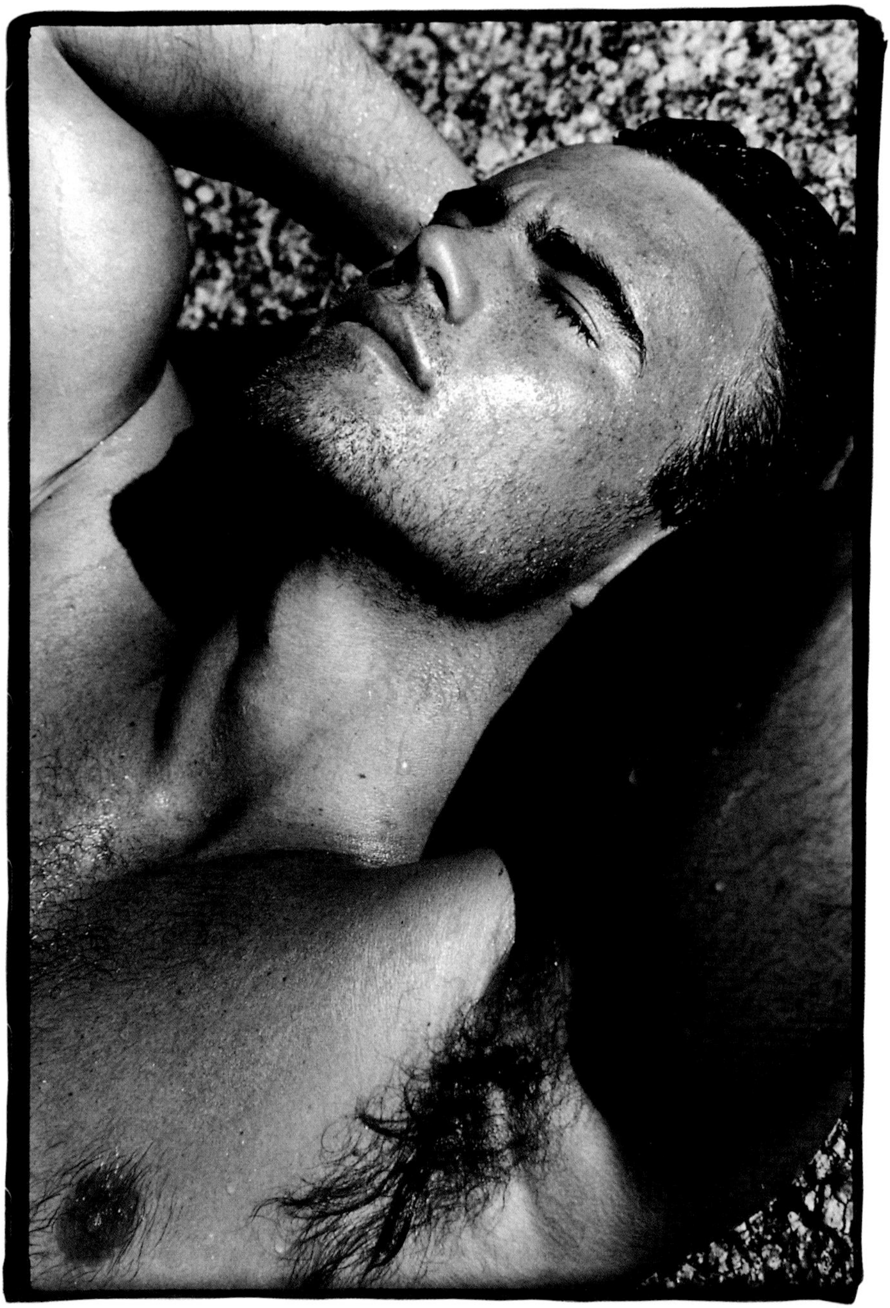

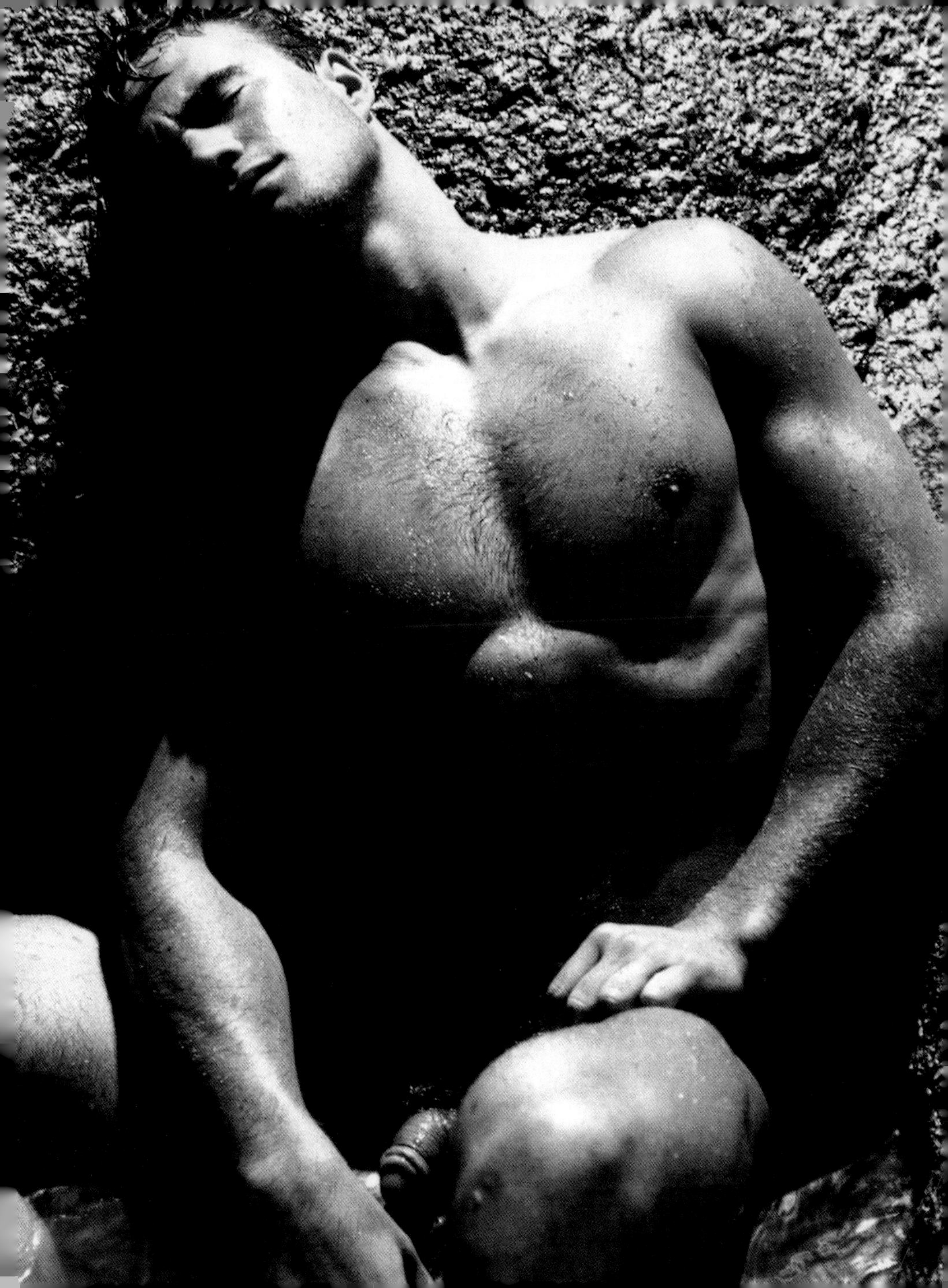

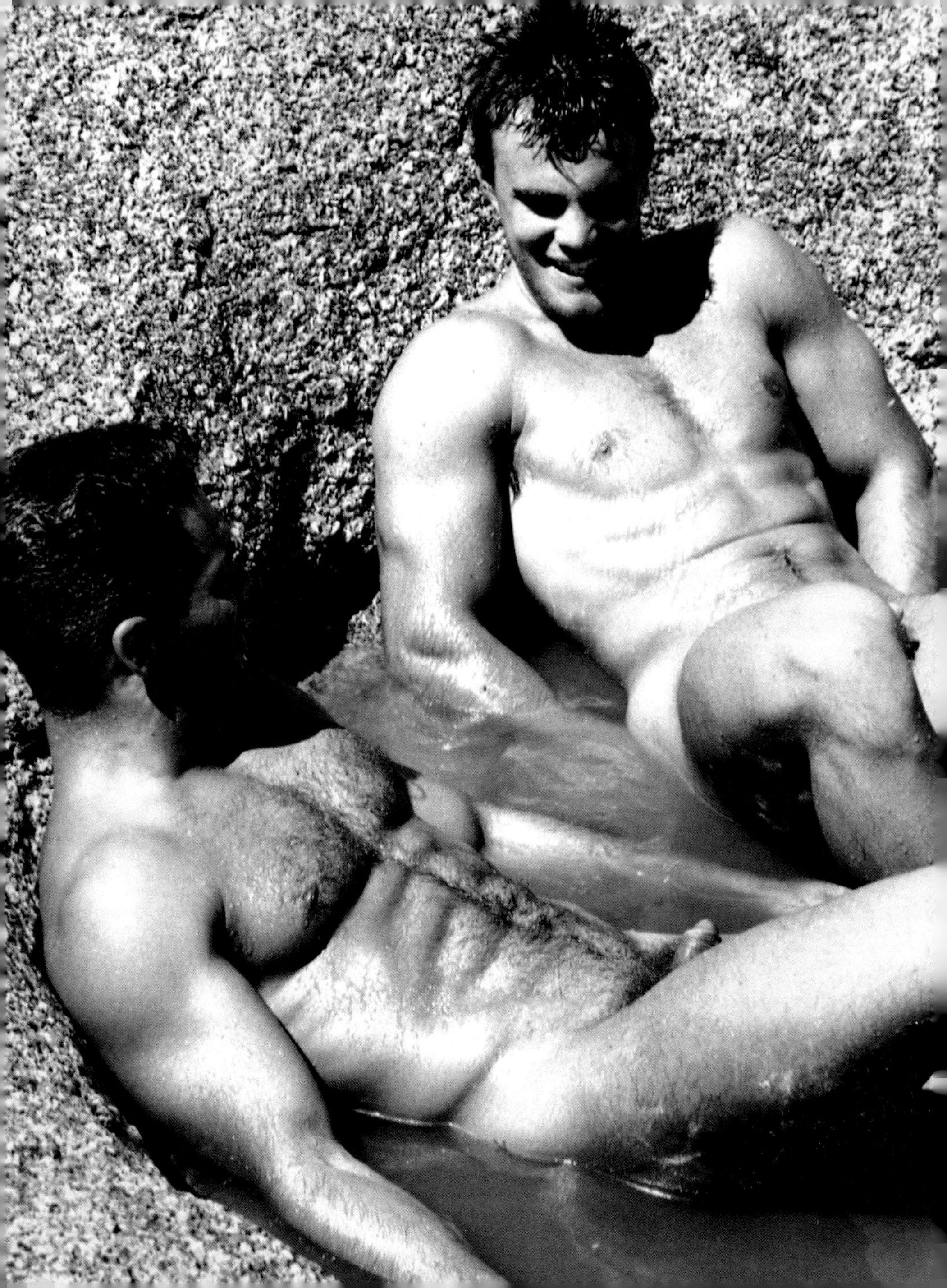

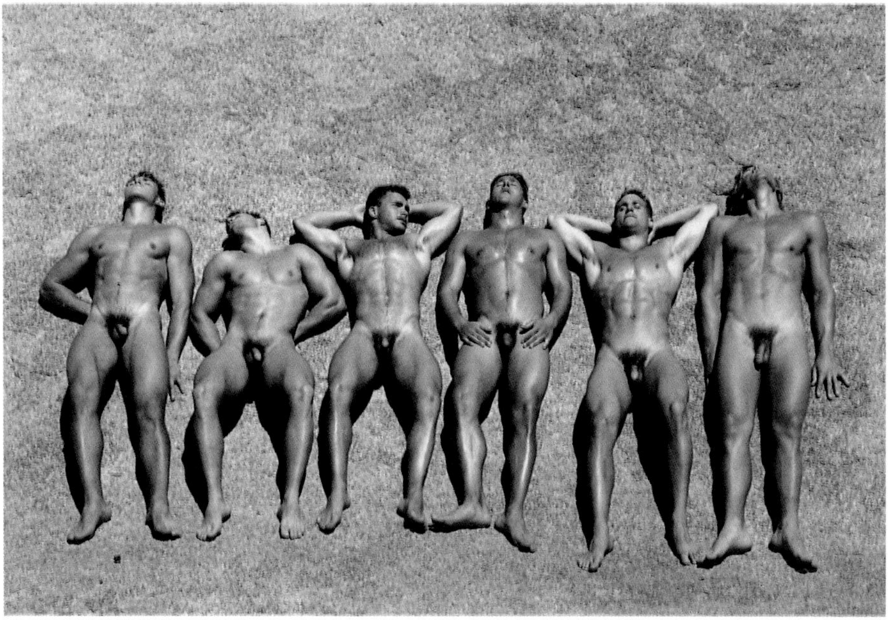

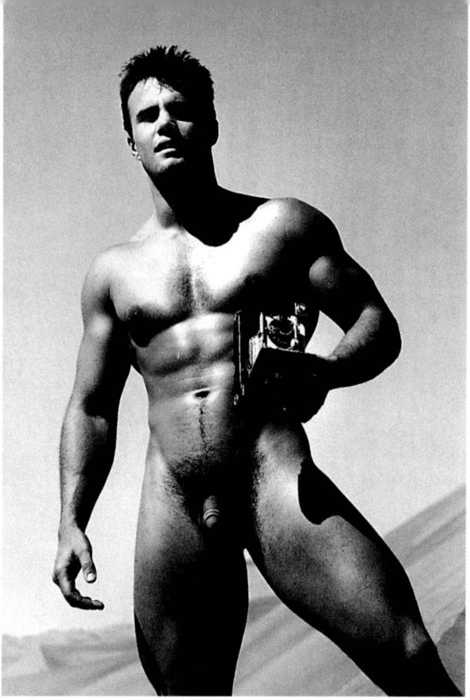

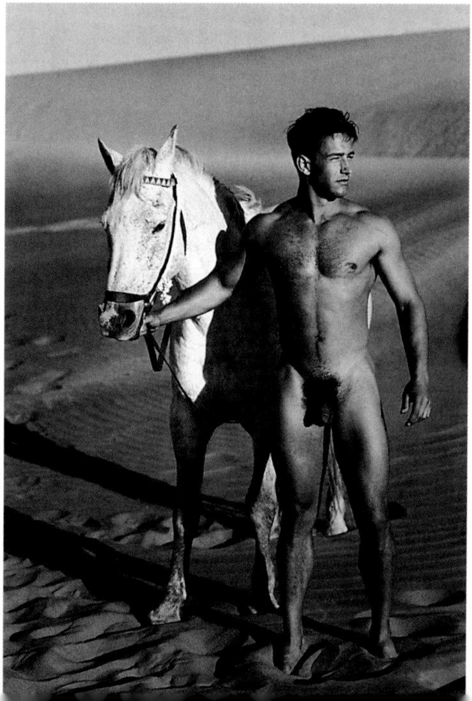

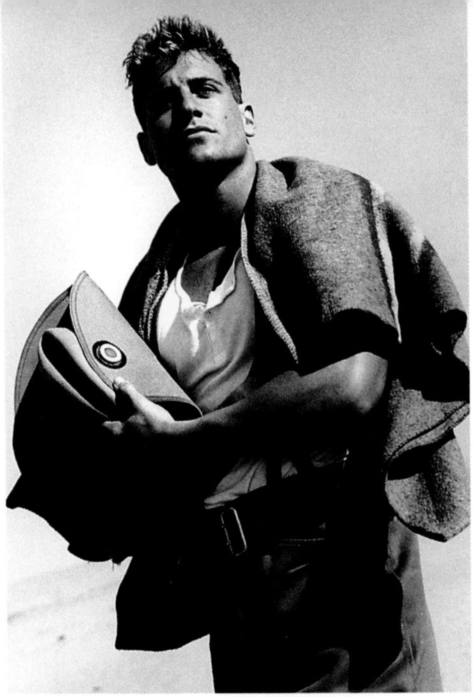

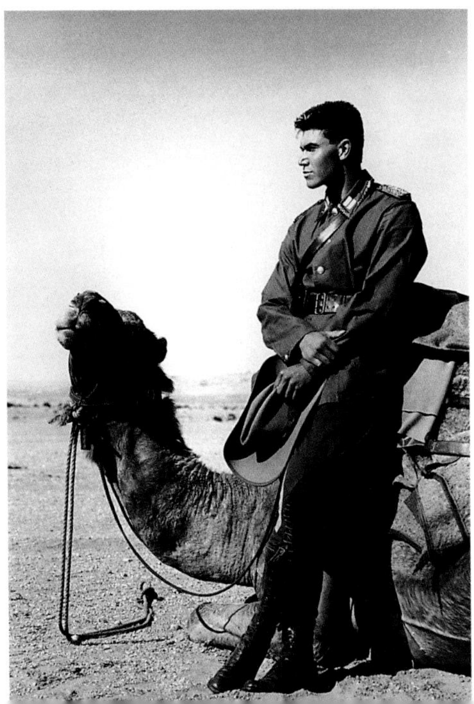

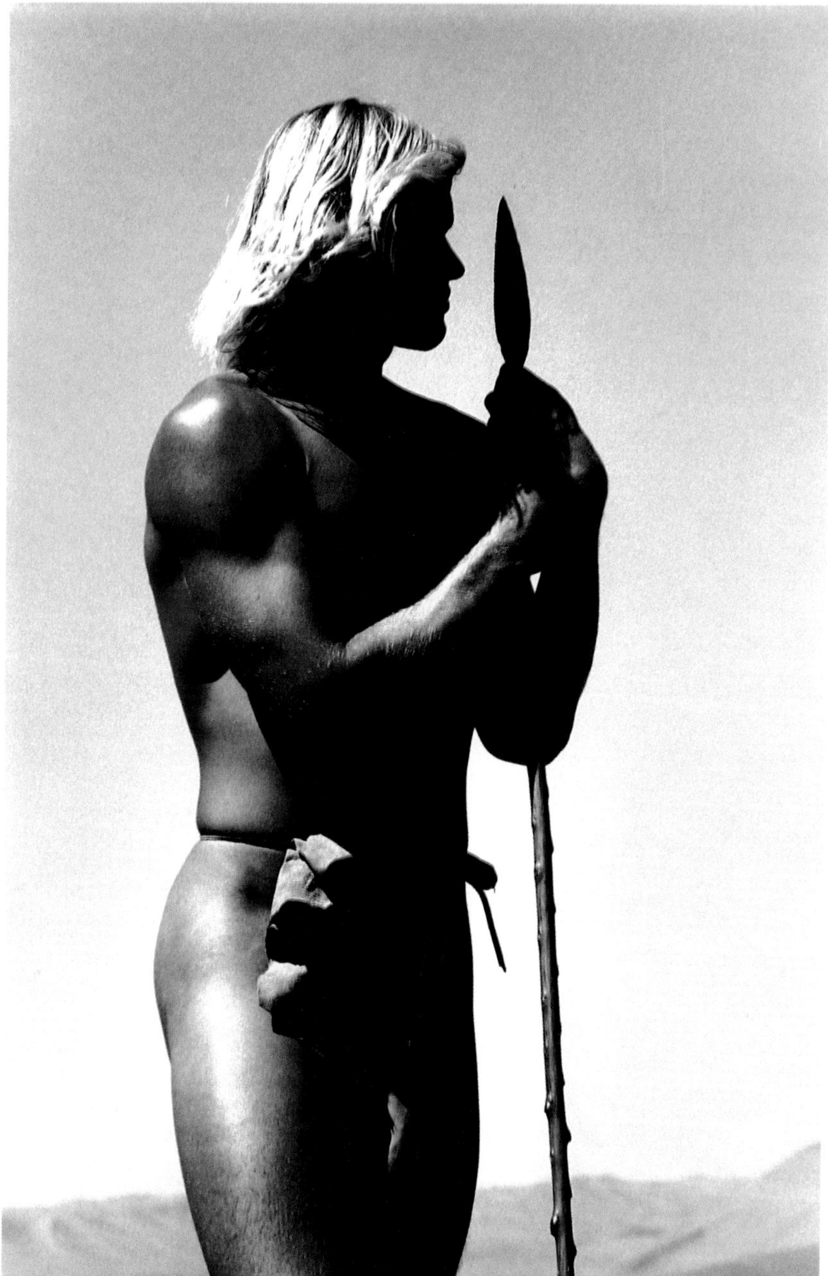

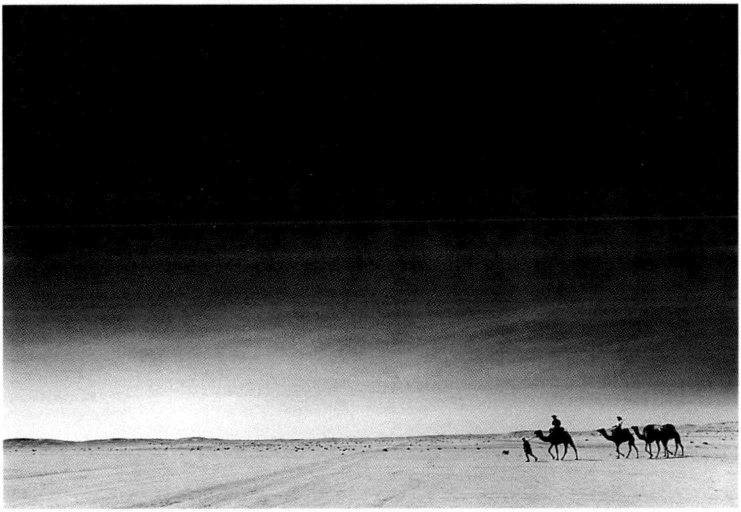

Bisher sind in der Reihe EDITION EUROS erschienen:

EDITION EUROS Nr 1
Clifford Baker
15 x 19 cm, 60 Seiten, ca 50 Bildtafeln.
Druck in Duoton, Hardcover.
ISBN 3-86187-061-4
22,80 DM

EDITION EUROS Nr 2
Mark Brickell
15 x 19 cm, 60 Seiten, ca 50 Bildtafeln.
Druck in Duoton, Hardcover.
ISBN 3-86187-062-2
22,80 DM

EDITION EUROS Nr 3
Benno Thoma
15 x 19 cm, 60 Seiten, ca 50 Bildtafeln.
Druck in Duoton, Hardcover.
ISBN 3-86187-072-X
22,80 DM

EDITION EUROS Nr 4
Andrew Melick
15 x 19 cm, 60 Seiten, ca 50 Bildtafeln.
Druck in Duoton, Hardcover.
ISBN 3-86187-073-8
22,80 DM

EDITION EUROS Nr 5
José Messana
15 x 19 cm, 60 Seiten, ca 50 Bildtafeln.
Druck in Duoton, Hardcover.
ISBN 3-86187-074-6
22,80 DM

EDITION EUROS Nr 6
Desert Patrol, Photographs by Dook
15 x 19 cm, 80 Seiten, ca 87 Bildtafeln.
Druck in Duoton, Hardcover.
ISBN 3-86187-075-4
26,80 DM

Bruno Gmünder Verlag
Postfach 11 07 29
10837 Berlin

EDITION EUROS

BRUNO GMÜNDER